COPYRIGHT

GW00514893

LIMITATION OF LIABILITY

Using The Resource Pack

Before working through this Spreadsheets resource pack 2, it is important you read the following information that has been written to offer you guidance on how to get the best out of these learning materials.

The resource pack has been divided into units, with each unit consisting of a number of related categories. Throughout these categories are tasks designed to underpin your knowledge of the categories. There are also references to theoretical knowledge that you will need to understand in order to create relevant and useful spreadsheet files.

If, when attempting the tasks, you need to refer back to the section you have just studied, don't worry - this will ensure you have the knowledge required before moving through the resource pack.

There are also consolidation exercises throughout the resource pack which will test your knowledge so far and which you should attempt to work through without reference. However, once again, if you find you are not sure of a particular section, do go back and work through it again.

Contents

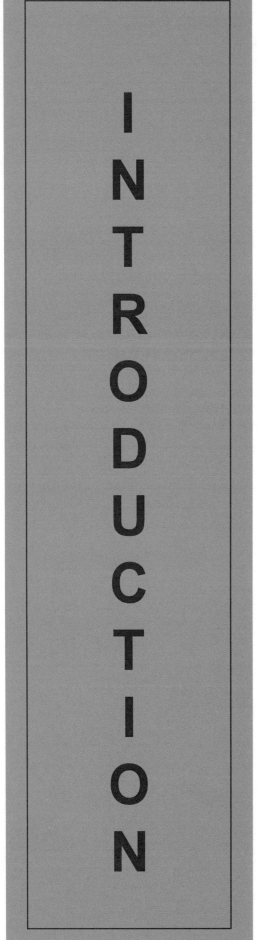

On completion of this introduction, you will have learnt about:

- **Introduction To Excel**

  - Useful Features
  - Types Of Information

Introduction To Excel

Excel is a very powerful spreadsheet application used to perform calculations quickly and accurately. The spreadsheet is referred to as a **worksheet** and several **worksheets** in one file are referred to as the **workbook.**

Useful Features

Recalculate data easily - When you update any data on the spreadsheet and it is set to automatic calculation, the entries are recalculated automatically.

Perform what-if analysis - One of Excel's most powerful functions is the ability to change data and immediately recalculate the changed results. Whenever a worksheet is used to answer the question "what if?", a what-if analysis is used. For example, if you wanted to see how much more your mortgage would cost if the rate went up, you enter the new rate in the spreadsheet and immediately see the results.

Changing the way information is presented - By using features such as bold, borders, Clip Art and shading, you can emphasise relevant information and present it in a visually appealing way.

Create charts - It is easy to create charts based on the information in a worksheet. When the information is changed, the chart is updated. Charts make data easier to interpret.

Create new workbooks from existing workbooks - You can modify an existing workbook to create a new one, or create a template to base all similar workbooks on.

Types Of Information

The three main types of information that can be used in spreadsheets are:

Labels	Usually text (eg headings) - text will be left-aligned by default but can be changed to centred or right-aligned. Text can be rotated and enhanced.
Values	This is the numeric data - the raw information fed into the spreadsheet. Figures will be right-aligned by default.
Formulae and functions	Formulae are the instructions given to the program enabling it to perform calculations for the user. Functions are predefined formulae that perform calculations by using specific values called arguments, ie the SUM function.

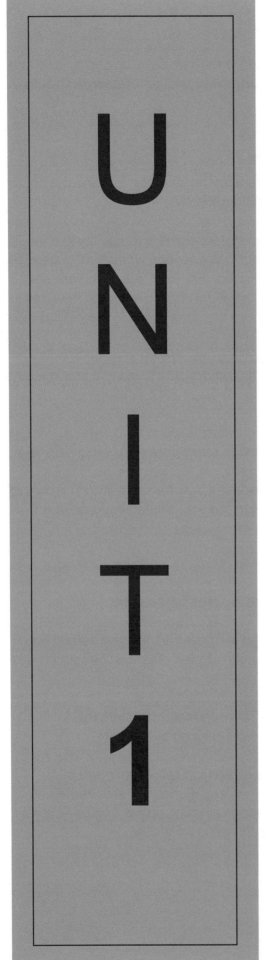

This unit will reintroduce you to Excel and some of its familiar features:

- **Basic Concepts**

  - Starting Excel
  - The Microsoft Excel 2000 Window
  - Selecting Individual Cells
  - Selecting Groups Of Cells
  - Selecting Unconnected Cells
  - Editing A Cell
  - Deleting Cells
  - Adjusting Column Width And Row Height
  - Adjusting The Width Of A Column
  - Adjusting The Height Of A Row
  - Saving A Worksheet
  - Closing A Workbook
  - Exiting From Excel
  - Opening An Existing Workbook

Basic Concepts

Starting Excel

Click the **Start** button on the Windows taskbar, point to **Programs** and click **Microsoft Excel**. Alternatively, you can double-click on the Microsoft Excel shortcut on the desktop, if you have one.

The Microsoft Excel 2000 Window

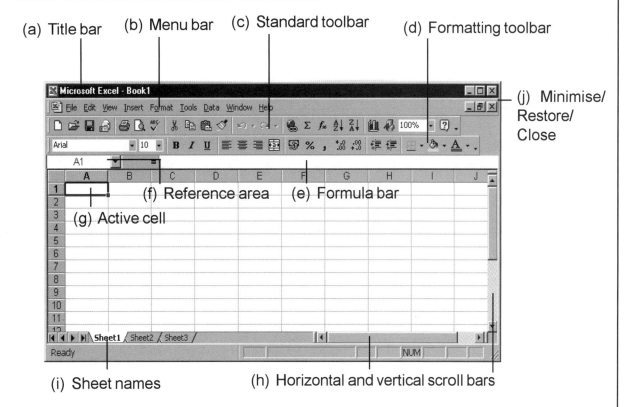

(a) Title bar   (b) Menu bar   (c) Standard toolbar   (d) Formatting toolbar

(j) Minimise/ Restore/ Close

(f) Reference area   (e) Formula bar

(g) Active cell

(i) Sheet names   (h) Horizontal and vertical scroll bars

a **Title bar**

The title bar shows the application you are working in, ie Excel and the name of the file. When you first open a workbook, the file is given a temporary name - Book 1, Book 2 etc.

b **Menu bar**

This bar contains menus, such as **File**, **Edit**, **View** etc. Clicking on one of these activates a drop-down menu containing various commands.

c **Standard toolbar**

Picture icons (or buttons) for commonly used commands are available on this toolbar to save time going into menus.

d **Formatting toolbar**

Picture icons (or buttons) for commonly used formatting commands. This saves time going into the **Format** menu. Format commands allow you to alter the appearance and alignment of data on your worksheet.

e **Formula bar**

Shows the contents of the active cell, which can then be edited on the formula bar.

f **Reference area**

Shows the cell reference of the active cell or the name of a selected range of cells, if a name has been assigned.

g **Active cell**

The cell currently selected is shown by a heavy border. On the previous page, the active cell in the screen shot is **A1**. You can only enter or edit data in the active cell.

h **Horizontal and vertical scroll bars**

The scroll bars allow you to move around a worksheet. The area that you can see on the screen at any time is only a small part of the entire worksheet.

i **Sheet names**

A new workbook consists of a number of blank worksheets. Each sheet is given a default name - Sheet 1, Sheet 2 etc until it is renamed. The sheet name in bold is the active sheet. (The sheet tab also displays as white.) On the previous page, the active sheet in the screen is Sheet 1.

j **Minimise/Restore/Close**

The worksheet can be set as a window within the application. To do this, click the **Restore** button. This is done by clicking the **Restore** button. To return to full screen view, click the same button to maximise the worksheet. To minimise the window to the foot of the screen, click the **Minimise** button. To close the worksheet, click the **Close** button.

| **T A S K** | 1. | *Open a blank workbook in Microsoft Excel 2000.* |
| | 2. | *Familiarise yourself with the components of the window.* |

Selecting Individual Cells

Change the active cell by either using the mouse to click into a different cell or by using the arrow keys on the keyboard to move to the cell that you wish to become the active cell. Alternatively, press **F5** to use the **Go To** facility, type the cell reference in the **Reference** box and press **Enter**.

Selecting Groups Of Cells

Using the mouse, click into the first cell of the range you wish to select. Hold down the left mouse button and drag the pointer down and across until all the cells required are highlighted. Clicking anywhere else on the worksheet will de-select the range. Note that the first cell selected (in this case the upper left-hand cell) will remain clear and your highlighting will always be in a block, ie square or rectangular.

Selecting Unconnected Cells

To select unconnected cells, select the first range and then hold down the **Ctrl** key on the keyboard. You can now select other, unconnected ranges on the worksheet.

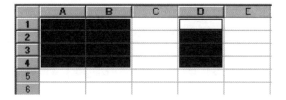

Editing A Cell

To edit a cell, whether it is a label, value or formula, you must first select the cell. If you are replacing all the contents of the cell, you can just type and the original contents will be replaced. If you wish to edit the data within the cell, you must either double-click on the cell, or press **F2** to change to edit mode. You can now make your alterations and press **Enter** to leave the cell. You can also edit a cell on the formula bar. This is often easier as there is more space and you can see the entire contents of the cell.

Deleting Cells

To clear the entire contents of a cell, click on the cell and press **Delete** on the keyboard, or chose **Edit**, **Clear**, **Contents** from the menu bar.

TASK

1. *Enter the data below into a blank worksheet.*

	A	B	C	D	E	F	G
1	Staff Overtime						
2							
3	Staff name	Payroll Number	Monda	Tuesday	Wednesda	Thursday	Friday
4	Davies, P						
5	Rodkinson, R						
6	Hallum, F						
7	Roger, F						
8	Jones, T						
9							

NB *Do not worry if you cannot see all the cell data (contents). Resizing columns is covered on the next page.*

Adjusting Column Width And Row Height

It may be necessary to adjust columns widths and/or row heights to accommodate the data you wish to type into the column or row. For example, in the **Staff Rota** worksheet the word 'Wednesday' (**E3**) is obscured as the column is not wide enough to display the whole word.

By default, columns on a worksheet are set to a standard size of 8.43 characters wide and rows are set to a standard size of 12.75 point size.

Adjusting The Width Of A Column

A column can be 'resized' to the required width.
Move the mouse pointer to the right of the column letter onto the border between the two columns. The mouse pointer changes to a double-headed arrow. Click and drag the mouse left or right to increase or decrease the column width. The current width of the column displays above the mouse. As the mouse is dragged, the measurement will change.

Alternatively, move the mouse pointer to the right of the column letter. When the mouse pointer changes to a double-headed arrow, double-click the mouse. The column will Autofit to the widest entry in the column.

The column width can also be changed using the **Column Width** dialogue box (this can be useful if you wish to change the width of multiple columns). Select the column or columns you wish to resize. Choose **Format** on the menu bar and click on **Column**, **Width**.

The following dialogue box will appear: ──────────

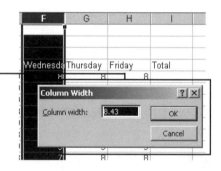

Type in the required measurement (in characters) and click **OK**.

©Tektra TEKSS2RP1102

Adjusting The Height Of A Row

A row can be 'resized' to the required height. Move the
mouse pointer to the bottom of the row number onto the border
between the two rows. The mouse pointer changes to a
double-headed arrow. Click and drag the mouse up or
down to increase or decrease the row height.
The current height of the row displays above the
mouse. As the mouse is dragged, the measurement
will change.

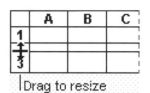

Alternatively, move the mouse pointer to the bottom of the row number. When the mouse
pointer changes to a double-headed arrow, double-click. The row will Autofit to the tallest
entry in the row.

The row height can also be changed using the
Row Height dialogue box (this can be useful if you
wish to change the height of multiple rows). Select
the row or rows you wish to resize. Choose
Format on the menu bar and click on **Row**, **Height**.

The following dialogue box will appear:

Type in the required measurement (in point size)
and click **OK**.

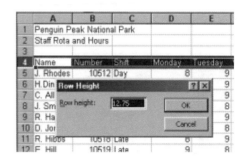

Saving A Worksheet

To reduce the risk of losing any data, save your work regularly. Choose **File** on the menu
bar and then click on **Save**, or press the **Save** button on the Standard toolbar.

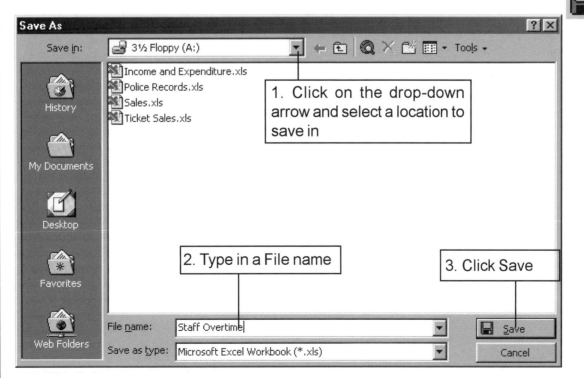

Closing A Workbook

It is important to close a workbook when you have finished working with it. This will eliminate the possibility of errors occurring.

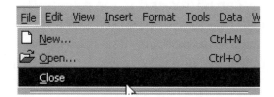

Choose **File**, **Close** from the menu bar

or

click the lower cross in the right-hand corner of the spreadsheet.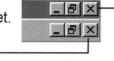

Exiting From Excel

The top cross will close the program. If you have not saved your work, you will be prompted to do so before Excel closes.

T A S K

1. Save the active workbook as **Staff Overtime** to your floppy disk.

2. Close the workbook.

Opening An Existing Workbook

To open an existing workbook, click **File**, **Open** from the menu bar to display the **Open** dialogue box.

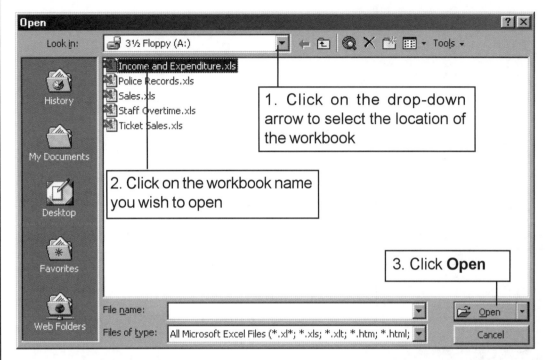

Click on the **Look in:** drop-down arrow to open a list containing the different drives. You may often use a floppy disk, usually known as the **A:** drive, but there are other drives available to you.

The **C:** drive is the hard disk drive - located in the system unit of the computer. Other available drives may include a **CD-ROM** drive or **DVD** drive.

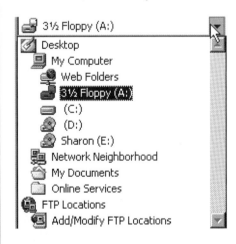

In this example, there are four drive letters, **A, C, D** and **E**, as well as other locations. The **D:** drive is usually a CD-ROM drive and the **E:** drive is usually a recordable CD writer.

Network Neighbourhood is used when connected to a network. You may store your work on a network drive.

My Documents (on the hard drive) is a shortcut to a folder where you can store your work.

T	1.	*Open an existing workbook called **Police Records** from your floppy disk.*
A		
S	2.	*View the worksheet.*
K		
	3.	*Close the workbook. If prompted click **No** to saving any changes.*

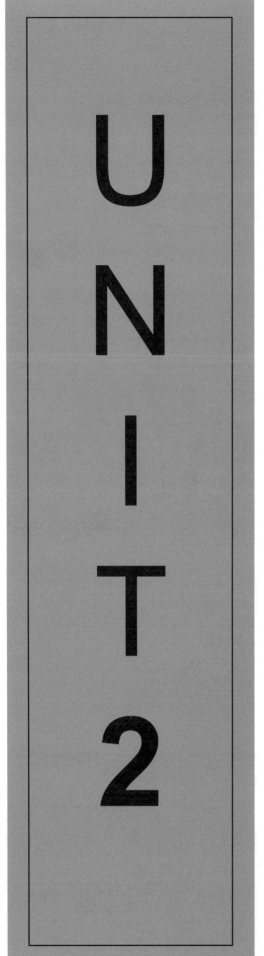

On completion of this unit, you will have learnt about and practised the following:

- **Adding Headers and Footers**

- **Printing**

  - Printing Sections Of A Worksheet
  - Setting A Print Area
  - Printing Formulae
  - Printing Titles, Row And Column Headings

- **Other Page Setup Options**

Adding Headers And Footers

A header is used to display information at the top of the worksheet when printed. A footer is used in the same way to display information at the bottom of a worksheet when printed. By including information such as the workbook or worksheet name, spreadsheets can be easily identifiable when they are printed out. Custom information can also be added to a header and/or footer such as a company name or an author's name.

T A S K

1. Open the spreadsheet *Income and Expenditure*.

Click **File**, **Page Setup** from the menu bar. This will display the **Page Setup** dialogue box. Select the **Header/ Footer** tab.

Choose a header and/ or footer from the drop-down lists or create a custom header or custom footer.

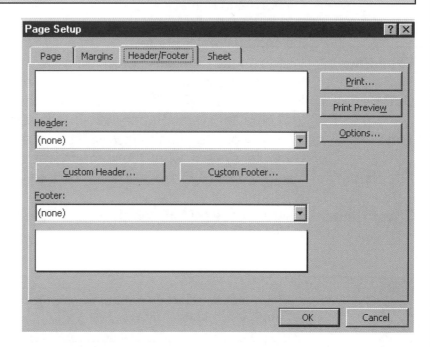

Click **Custom Header** or **Custom Footer** to display the corresponding dialogue box.

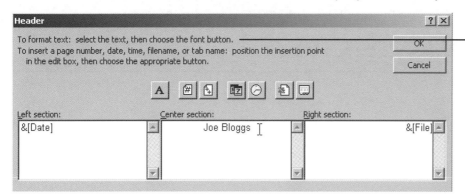

Headers can contain information aligned left, centre and right. Enter the required text into the appropriate section. Text can be typed directly into each section by clicking the left mouse button in the section and typing. You can also use the buttons to insert codes. The header dialogue contains information on how to do this.

To delete, click into the section, highlight the text and press **Delete** on the keyboard.

Preset buttons

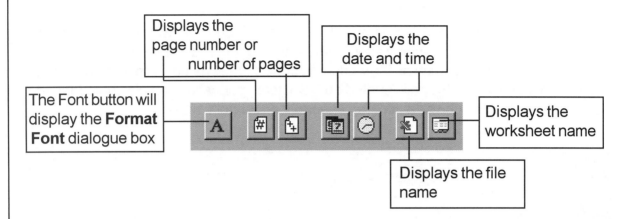

Displays the page number or number of pages

Displays the date and time

The Font button will display the **Format Font** dialogue box

Displays the worksheet name

Displays the file name

Font	This will open the **Font** dialogue box. You can select text in any of the sections and format it.
Page Number	Inserts a code (&[Page]) which will show the current page number when the spreadsheet is printed.
Total Pages	Inserts a code (&[Pages]) which will show the total number of pages when the spreadsheet is printed.
Date	Inserts a code (&[Date]) which will show the current date (according to the computer system) when the spreadsheet is printed.
Time	Inserts a code (&[Time]) which will show the current time (according to the computer system) when the spreadsheet is printed.
File Name	Inserts a code (&[File]) which will show the file name when the spreadsheet is printed.
Sheet Name	Inserts a code (&[Tab]) which will show the sheet name when the spreadsheet is printed.

TASK

1. *Create a custom header. In the left section put the date. In the centre section, type your name. In the right section, enter the file name. Click **OK** to come out of **Page Setup** box.*

2. *Print preview the spreadsheet, then close the print preview.*

3. *Save the changes to the spreadsheet.*

Printing

Printing Sections Of A Worksheet

If only certain cells in a worksheet are required to be printed, it is possible to print only the selection. To do this, select the cells you wish to print.

Click **File**, **Print** from the menu bar to display the **Print** dialogue box.

Note: the name of your printer may be different.

Click on the **Selection** button in the **Print what** section and Click **OK**.

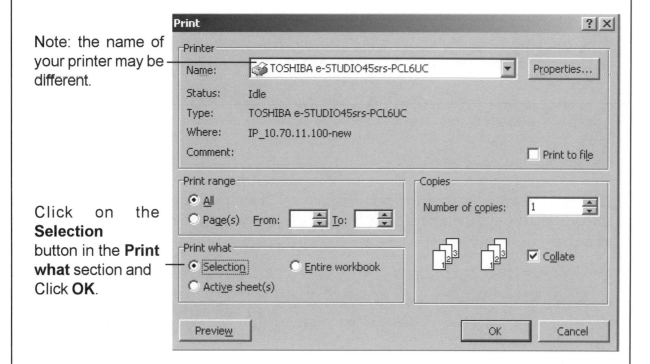

Setting A Print Area

If a specific section of a worksheet is required for printing all the time, you can set it as a print area. This will mean that whenever that worksheet is printed, the section that was set as the print area will print.

Select the cell range that is required for printing and click **File**, **Print Area**, **Set Print Area** from the menu bar.

To clear the print area, click **File**, **Print Area**, **Clear Print Area** from the menu bar.

TASK

1. Set the print area in the **Income and Expenditure** spreadsheet to print out the expenditure for **January**.

2. Print preview to check the correct information is displayed and print out one copy.

Print preview will only show the cells that are set in the print area. To view the entire spreadsheet but with the print area highlighted, click **View**, **Page Break Preview** from the menu bar.

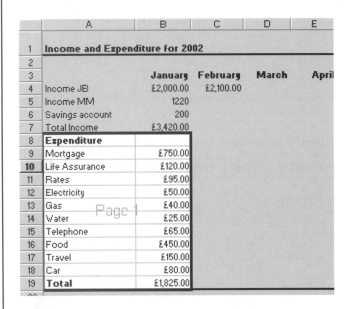

You can increase the print area by pointing to any edge of the existing print area and clicking and dragging the print area borders to a new position.

Click **View**, **Normal** from the menu bar to return to Normal view.

TASK

1. Switch to **Page Break Preview**.

2. Extend the print area to include February.

3. Print out the new print area.

4. Save the changes.

©Tektra TEKSS2RP1102

Printing Formulae

When working in spreadsheets which include formulae, it may be necessary to view the formulae used in the spreadsheet. There may be calculations on the worksheet which are not immediately apparent. To view the formulae, click **Tools**, **Options** from the menu bar and click on the **View** tab.

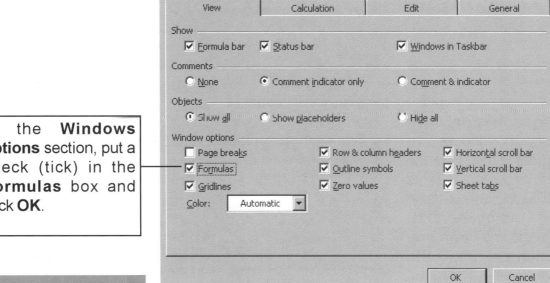

In the **Windows options** section, put a check (tick) in the **Formulas** box and click **OK**.

An alternative method is to hold down the **Ctrl** key and press the left accent key above the Tab key `.

To switch off formulae view, either remove the tick from the **Formulas** box in the **Options** dialogue box or repeat the alternative method.

T A S K

1. Show the formulae in the *Income and Expenditure* spreadsheet.

2. Print income and expenditure for *January* and *February*, showing the formulae.

3. Clear any print areas.

4. Hide the formulae.

5. Save the changes.

Printing Titles, Row And Column Headings

A large spreadsheet, even if printed in landscape mode, may print out onto more than one page. It is useful to have your row and column headings showing on each page.

Click **File**, **Page Setup** from the menu bar to open the **Page Setup** dialogue box. Select the **Sheet** tab.

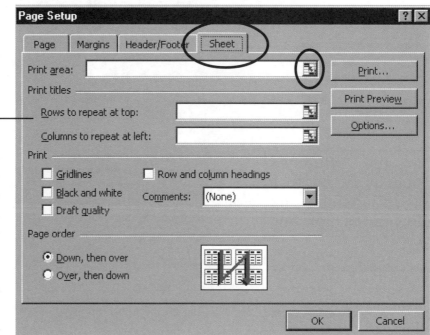

Click in the **Print titles** section, **Rows to repeat at top**. Click the red arrow icon. (This will temporarily collapse the dialogue box). Select the rows you require on the worksheet. These will then be displayed in the box.

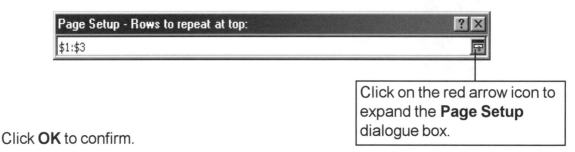

Click on the red arrow icon to expand the **Page Setup** dialogue box.

Click **OK** to confirm.

Repeat this procedure to set the columns to repeat at left.

T A S K

1. *Select rows **1** to **3** to repeat at the top.*

2. *Select column **A** to repeat at left.*

3. *Print preview the spreadsheet and check that the rows and columns are appearing correctly.*

4. *Print the spreadsheet.*

5. *Save the changes.*

Other Page Setup Options

Other options in the **Sheet** tab of the **Page Setup** dialogue box include the option to print gridlines, print in black and white, print the row and column headings (ie the rows numbers and column letters) and to print in Draft quality.

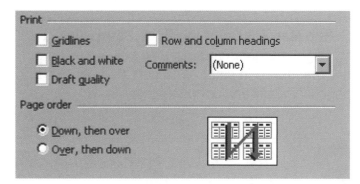

Print

Gridlines are the grey lines that appear across the whole worksheet on the screen. If you check this box, a grid of thin black lines will be printed across the page.

If you have created a colour worksheet and you print to a colour printer, but only want a black and white print-out, check the **Black and white** box.

If you want a quick print-out of the raw data, without seeing formatting or graphics, you can check the **Draft quality** box.

If you wish to see the row and column headings (ie column letters across the top and row headings down the left side), check the **Row and column headings** box.

If you have entered comments onto the worksheet (**Insert**, **Comment**) and you wish to print the comments, choose the option you require from the **Comments** drop-down list.

Page order

If your worksheet will print onto more than one page, you can choose the order in which the worksheet should print onto the pages. (If you have page numbers appearing in a header or footer, it is important that the pages print in the correct order.)

The scaling section of the **Page** tab in the **Page Setup** dialogue box allows you to adjust the scale of a spreadsheet. This may be necessary if you wish to adjust the size of the spreadsheet to fit onto the printed page.

The **Fit to** option allows you to specify that a spreadsheet fits onto a specified number of pages wide by a specified number of pages tall.

You can also set the page orientation (portrait or landscape) on the **Page** tab of the **Page Setup** dialogue box. Portrait will print the short edge of the paper at the top. Landscape will print the long edge of the paper at the top.

On the **Margins** tab of the **Page Setup** dialogue box you can adjust the top, bottom, left and right margins. You can also adjust the margin for the header and footer (the margins are measured in cms). You can also choose to centre the spreadsheet on the printed page, vertically and/or horizontally.

<table>
<tr>
<td>T
A
S
K</td>
<td>1.</td>
<td>*In your **Income and Expenditure** spreadsheet (in no particular order), set the following:*

Print gridlines
Format to landscape orientation
Print row and column headings
Fit to one page wide by one page tall
Add a custom footer in the left section: **Spreadsheets Resources 2**</td>
</tr>
<tr>
<td></td>
<td>2.</td>
<td>*Print the spreadsheet.*</td>
</tr>
<tr>
<td></td>
<td>3.</td>
<td>*Save the changes.*</td>
</tr>
<tr>
<td></td>
<td>4.</td>
<td>*Close the worksheet.*</td>
</tr>
</table>

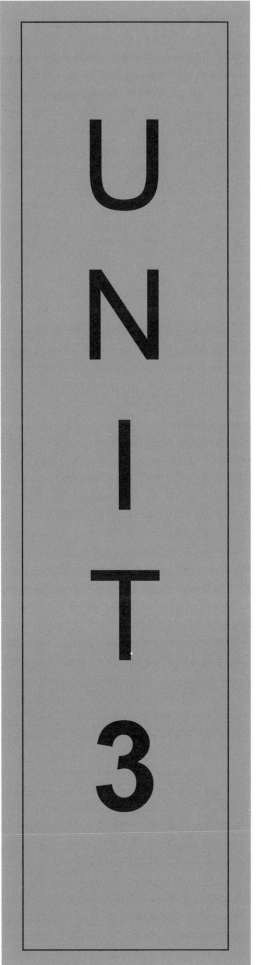

On completion of this unit, you will have learnt about and practised the following:

- **Designing, Creating and Testing A Spreadsheet**

  - Types Of Data
  - Protected And Hidden Cells
  - Creating Test Data To Validate The Spreadsheet Independently
  - Types of Test Data Used To Validate
  - Step 1 - Designing A Spreadsheet (Sketch)
  - Creating A Data Input Form
  - Step 2 - Creating The Spreadsheet From A Given Design
  - Setting Properties
  - Adding And Removing Gridlines
  - Formatting Cells

Designing, Creating And Testing A Spreadsheet

Many of the spreadsheets you create may be small and uncomplicated. This may mean that the information can be input directly onto the worksheet. However, when you are planning a more complex spreadsheet using many formulae and functions and involving many calculations, it is a good idea to use the **Design**, **Create** and **Test** procedure.

> **Step 1** is the **Design**, which involves planning the purpose and layout of the spreadsheet, ie what it will be used for and how it will look. This will involve producing a sketch. This stage will also involve the creation of a **Data Input Form** (refer to the example below).
>
> **Step 2** is **Create**, ie the design (sketch) is taken to the computer and input onto a spreadsheet.
>
> **Step 3** is **Test**, ie a small amount of test data (one or two rows) is input onto the spreadsheet to arrive at a result(s) in a cell(s). The calculations are tested on a calculator manually and compared against the result on the computer.

> **The following is an example scenario demonstrating why the Design, Create and Test Procedure is used:**

Mr Jones owns a fruit and veg cash and carry, together with 15 fruit and veg market stalls located across the Midlands.

Every Friday Mr Jones travels around to each of his market stalls to take his market traders' orders for the following week. The market traders do not have access to a computer and so all requirements are put onto paper. For this purpose, Mr Jones created a Data Input Form, which can be used by each of his market traders.

After visiting all of the 15 market stalls, Mr Jones has 15 Data Input Forms for the following week's requirements. The Data Input Form contains information such as:

> The market trader's name
> The market trader's location
> The date
> A table which lists all produce (such as oranges, apples etc)

Each market trader will enter the required amount of produce against each item.

Mr Jones has designed a spreadsheet so that he can easily transfer the information from the Data Input Form and automatically work out how much produce is required in total and what produce he will have left in stock, so that he can re-order.

Mr Jones carefully planned the design of the spreadsheet he required and this included considerations such as which columns and rows contained which information, what font size would be appropriate and what formulae and functions he should use to get the desired results.

Careful planning of a spreadsheet will be necessary to obtain the correct results.

Types Of Data

There are two types of input data, **constant input data** and **variable input data**. Constant input data is usually headings, labels, titles etc, which do not change when more information is added. Variable input data can change from day to day, week to week etc.

Output data is the data resulting from the processing of information, ie results of formulae and functions. This is often known as **data processing.**

Income and Expenditure for 2002

	January	
Income JB	£2,000.00	← Variable input data
Income MM	1220	
Savings account	200	
Total Income	£3,420.00	← Output data
Expenditure		
Mortgage	£750.00	
Life Assurance	£120.00	
Rates	£95.00	← Variable input data
Electricity	£50.00	
Gas	£40.00	
Water	£25.00	
Telephone	£65.00	
Food	£450.00	
Travel	£150.00	
Car	£80.00	
Total	£1,825.00	← Output data

Constant input data ← (Income JB through Water labels)

The output data in the above example are the Total Income and Total Expenditure amounts. Both figures have been calculated by using the SUM function.

Protected And Hidden Cells

When a cell is protected, it stops a user of the spreadsheet from typing in it. It is good practice to protect all the cells on the spreadsheet apart from those that require variable input data.

You can hide cells so that they cannot be seen when the spreadsheet is viewed. For example, if your spreadsheet was used to calculate total earnings, or sales totals, or other data that could be sensitive, this data could be hidden.

For instructions on how to hide rows or columns see page 61.

Creating Test Data To Validate The Spreadsheet Independently

This is Step 3 in the Design, Create and Test process. If you are creating a spreadsheet with multiple calculations, enter some 'test' data. Use a calculator to see if the functions and formulas calculate correctly.

Types Of Test Data Used To Validate

If you had to find the percentage number of passes, credits and distinctions from a set of music examinations for 185 students when 85 got a pass, 55 received credits and 45 got distinctions, your formulae would be similar to:

=Pass/Exams taken
=Credit/Exams taken
=Distinction/Exams taken

	A	B	C	D
1	Exams taken	Pass	Credit	Distinction
2	185	85	55	45
3				
4	Percentage	45.95%	29.73%	24.32%

The data has been entered into this spreadsheet and the formulae have been written. The formulae are:
=B2/A2
=C2/A2
=D2/A2

Percentage formatting (with 2 decimal places) has then been applied to the results.

The number of Passes, Credits and Distinctions should always = the number of exams taken. The percentages should always = 100%.

If you change the number of passes to 95, then the total of Passes, Credits and Distinctions is now greater than the number of exams taken and the percentage calculations will total more than 100%.

It is always useful to check calculations on a calculator to ensure that you have written the correct formula.

<u>Step 1 - Designing A Spreadsheet (Sketch)</u>

Step 1 is the design of the spreadsheet. Make a decision on the purpose and general layout and consider the following:

1   The purpose of the worksheet. Decide on a suitable name relevant to the contents.

2   Identify the constant input data, variable input data and what data will be generated by data processing to give output data.

3   What calculations, ie formulae and/or functions will you need to achieve the output data?

4   Draw a sketch showing where your labels and titles will go. Show approximate widths of columns (which can be amended at the Create stage) and the formatting required, ie will the titles be in bold?

5   Give an idea of font size and font, ie Arial 24pt.

6   What areas of the spreadsheet should be protected so that constant input data and formulae will not be overwritten?

7   Do any cells need to be hidden?

8   Should the spreadsheet be printed in portrait or landscape orientation?

9   Produce a Data Input Form for the collection of input data.

10   Use test data to check if the formulae and functions work.

> The sketch overleaf is an example of the Design stage of a spreadsheet, incorporating all of the above points.

Example of how sketch might look

Survey of Local Restaurants (enlarge to font size 24)

Constant Input Data

Researchers name
ID
Date of Survey

Name Of Person
Address 1
Address 2
Town
Post Code
Telephone No.

Price Band
Views on
Location
Service
Value for money
Accomodation if available
Parking
Would you visit again?
(align this data right)
Format Column A to text

Variable Input Data

(should always be todays date)

Between 10 and 60
(centre align)

Output Data

Insert a function to show "Please enter name"
Insert a function to show "Please enter ID"
Insert a function to show "Please enter todays date"

Below 50 function to show "Family Rates"
Above 50 function to show "Too Expensive"

Notes :-
• Column widths set to 25
• Font Arial size 10
• Add shading and borders to make data stand out.
• Insert a function to show "Advise availability of discount" if person does not wish to give name OR "Give discount vouchers" if they do.
• All data protected except column B
• Format B3, B7:B12 to text, B4 to number, B5 to date and B14 to Currency.

Creating A Data Input Form

A Data Input Form can be produced using pencil and paper or using any application which you are comfortable with (eg Microsoft Word). When you are producing the Data Input Form, consider the scenario you have been given, ie what data are you collecting and how will it be transferred onto the spreadsheet?

For the example scenario given previously in which Mr Jones collects the data for his fruit and veg produce, the Data Input Form may look similar to this.

Data Input Form	
Weekly Fruit and Vegetable Requirements	
Name of Trader	
Location	
Date	
Produce	**Number Required**
Oranges	
Apples	
Bananas	
Broccoli	
Cauliflower	
Green Beans	
Pears	
Strawberries	

T A S K

The Scenario:

A market research company wish to carry out a survey of local restaurants. They will use a standard form for each person surveyed which will show:

Researcher's Name - should ask for name to be entered
ID - should ask for ID to be entered
Date of Survey (should always be today's date and ask for date to be entered)
Name of Person
Address 1
Address 2
Town
Post Code
Telephone No.

NB It is not mandatory for the person to give their name, but if they do they will be offered vouchers at their favourite restaurant; otherwise they will be informed of discount vouchers available.

Price Band - person will be asked to give a range between £10 and £60 (if the price is more than £50, screen will show 'Too Expensive'; otherwise it will show 'Family Rates'),
Views on:
Location
Service
Value for Money
Accommodation (if available)
Parking
Would you visit again?

T
A
S
K

1. Sketch out a design for the scenario given on the previous page.

2. Design a data input form relating to the scenario given on the previous page (this can be produced using word processor or sketched by hand).

Your data input form may look similar to this:

The Market Research Company

Data Input Form

Name of Person	
Address 1	
Address 2	
Town	
Post Code	
Telephone	
Price Band	
Views on:	
Location	
Service	
Value for Money	
Accommodation (if available)	
Parking	
Would you visit again?	

Step 2 - Creating The Spreadsheet From A Given Design

Now you can create your spreadsheet using your design (sketch) and your data input form. As you work through the different areas, you may see that perhaps your columns should be wider, or a larger font is more appropriate etc. The sketch is just a rough guide.

T A S K

1. *Launch Excel create a new blank spreadsheet.*

2. *Key in the following data into Sheet 1 in the font of your choice (this particular spreadsheet is using Arial 10pt). Ensure everything is entered in the same location as shown in the example below:*

	A	B	C
1	Survey on local restaurants		
2	by		
3	ID		
4	date		
5			
6			
7	Name of Person		
8	Address1		
9	Address2		
10	Town		
11	Post Code		
12	Telephone		
13			
14	Price Band		
15	Views on		
16	Location		
17	Service		
18	Value for Money		
19	Accommodation if available		
20	Parking		
21	Would you visit again?		

3. *Extend the column widths as necessary so that all of the text (except the main heading) fits into the cells. (Did you realise when you were designing your sketch that the title would span several columns?).*

4. *Save the spreadsheet with the name **Restaurant Survey 2002**.*

Setting Properties

When you are creating many spreadsheets, it is useful to set Properties so that if you forget the name or someone wishes to see who created the spreadsheet, this information is available.

Click **File**, **Properties** from the menu bar to open the **File Properties** dialogue box for this workbook.

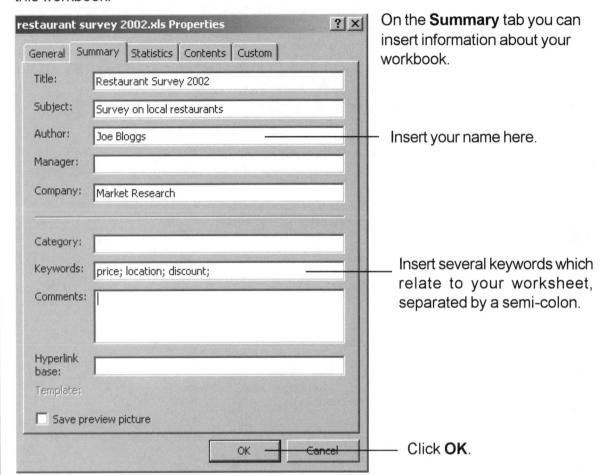

On the **Summary** tab you can insert information about your workbook.

Insert your name here.

Insert several keywords which relate to your worksheet, separated by a semi-colon.

Click **OK**.

T A S K

1. Set the properties of the **Restaurant Survey 2002** file just saved to show you are the author, together with the content of the spreadsheet and some appropriate key words.

Adding And Removing Gridlines

Each time you start a new workbook in Excel, gridlines will be displayed which define each cell. If preferred, it is possible to display a spreadsheet so the gridlines do not show.

Click **Tools**, **Options** from the menu bar. The **Options** dialogue box will be displayed.

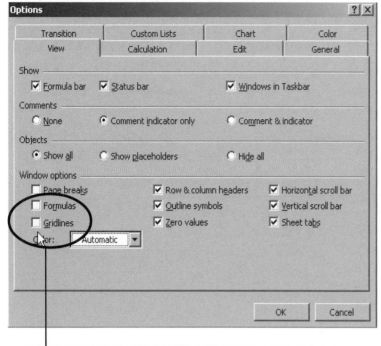

Click on the **View** tab.

Choose whether to view or hide the gridlines in a spreadsheet by checking or unchecking the **Gridlines** box in the **Window options** section of the dialogue box.

This will only view or hide the gridlines for the active worksheet.

You can choose to print a workbook or worksheet with or without gridlines using the checkbox option in the **Page Setup** dialogue box (**Sheet** tab).

When you remove the tick from the **Gridlines** box, your spreadsheet will appear similar to this:

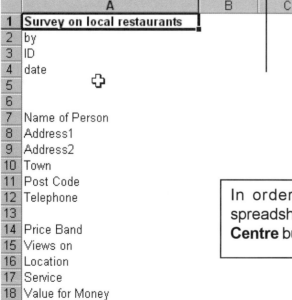

In order to centre your heading across the spreadsheet, A1:B1, then click on the **Merge and Centre** button.

	A	B	C
1		Survey on local restaurants	

Formatting Cells

An initial design (sketch) should include a rough idea of the formats required in cells. This can include: font colour, borders, alignment and types of data in each cell. One of the initial stages of creating the spreadsheet for use on the computer is the formatting of all cells, ready to receive their data.

To format cells, click **Format**, **Cells** from the menu bar. This will display the **Format Cells** dialogue box.

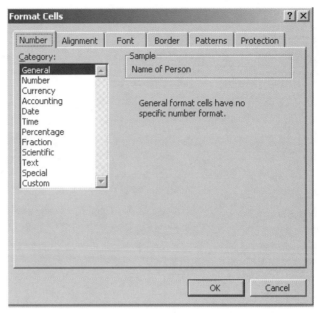

The **Number** tab will allow you to specify the type of data in each cell or range of cells.

Select the cell(s) before opening the dialogue box and select the category required, for example, to set date formatting, click on **Date** in the **Category** list and then select the date format you require from the **Type** list. Click **OK** to apply that formatting to the selected cells.

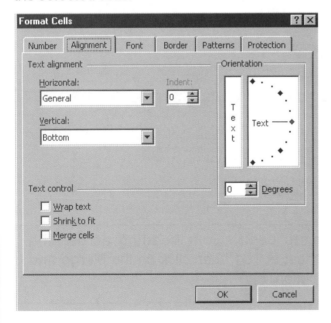

The **Alignment** tab allows you to set a specific alignment for each cell or range of cells. Text can also be set to appear slanted in orientation by clicking on the red diamond in the **Orientation** section of the dialogue box and dragging it to a different angle.

Text control allows you to wrap text within a cell, shrink it to fit inside a cell and merge cells.

Click **OK** to apply the settings.

©Tektra TEKSS2RP1102

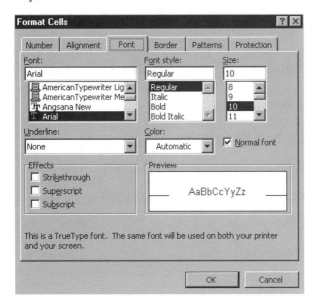

The **Font** tab enables you to change the font settings of text, ie the font type, style and size, and apply other effects to the text.

The text colour can also be changed by choosing a colour from the drop-down palette.

Click **OK** to apply the settings.

You can apply borders to cells using the **Border** tab. There are three sections: **Presets**, **Border** and **Line**.

Depending on the cell(s) selected on the spreadsheet, a preset will become available.

Choose a **Line Style** and a **Line Colour** and click on one of the presets or click on which border you want to apply. The preview window shows you what you have chosen.

Click **OK** to apply the settings.

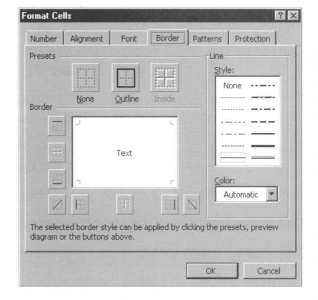

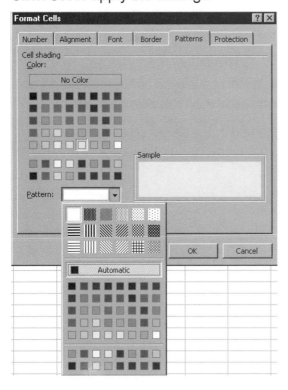

The **Patterns** tab allows you to change add shading or a pattern to a cell(s). Click on a cell shading colour to select it and a sample of the colour will appear in the **Sample** window.

If a pattern is required in a cell, click on the drop-down arrow to reveal the pattern palette. Choose a pattern and a pattern colour.

Click **OK** to apply the settings.

You can also use the Formatting toolbar to apply common formatting.

Font	Choose a font from the drop-down list
Font Size	Choose a font size from the drop-down list
Bold	Apply bold to selected cells by clicking on the **B** button
Italic	Apply italic to selected cells by clicking on the **I** button
Underline	Apply underline to selected cells by clicking on the **U** button
Align Left	Left align the contents of selected cells
Centre	Centre the contents of selected cells
Align Right	Right align the contents of selected cells
Merge and Centre	Merge selected cells and centre text in the merged cell
Currency	Apply currency (accounting) format to selected cells. (This will display £ sign, a thousand separator and two decimal places)
Percent Style	Apply percent style to selected cells (this will multiple the value by 100 and add a percent sign)
Comma Style	Apply comma style to selected cells (this will add a thousand separator and two decimal places)
Increase Decimal	Increase the number of decimal places of the selected cells
Decrease Decimal	Decrease the number of decimal places of the selected cells
Decrease Indent	Move the contents of selected cells back to the left side of the cell
Increase Indent	Move the contents of selected cells to the right, away from the left side of the cell
Borders	Apply the border shown to the selected cells (you can choose different borders from the border palette – click on the down arrow)
Fill Colour	Apply the colour shown to selected cells (you can choose different colours from the colour palette – click on the down arrow)
Font Colour	Apply the colour shown to the text in the selected cells (you can choose different colours from the colour palette – click on the down arrow)

**T
A
S
K**

1. From the **Restaurant Survey 2002** file, remove the gridlines.

2. Centre the heading across columns **A**-**C**.

3. Shade in all the cells of the form, except where data entry is required, in pale grey.

4. Shade the cells referring to the **Researcher** information (by ID and Date, ie **A1**,**A2** and **A3**) in a pale colour and shade the cells referring to personal data in a different colour.

5. Shade the cells for the responses in another pale colour or leave white.

6. Change the font size of the heading to 24 and change the font.

7. Widen columns **B** and **C** (if required) in order to display all data.

8. Use print preview to ensure the spreadsheet fits on one page.

9. Format the cells as per your design, ie:

> Column **A** - text
> Cells **B2** and **B7** to **B12** - text
> Cell **B3** - number, 0 decimal places
> Cell **B4** - date
> Cell **B14** - currency, 2 decimal places

10. Print preview and check for overall layout, adjust where necessary.

11. Print in landscape orientation.

12. Check your sketch is showing any improvements you have now made.

13. Save the changes to your spreadsheet.

14. Close the spreadsheet.

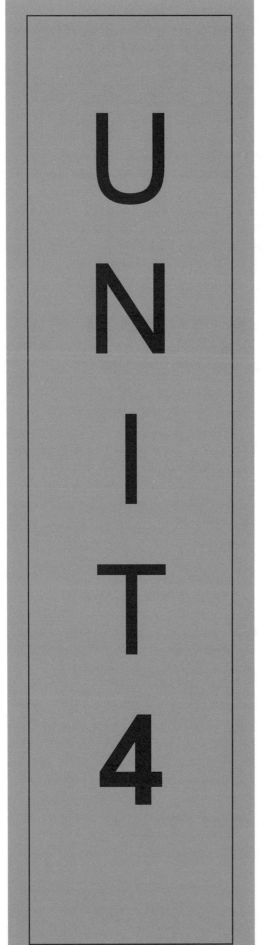

On completion of this unit, you will have learnt about and practised the following:

- **Automatic Data Validation**

  - Validating Data
  - Validation Error Messages
  - Using IF Functions For Validation

- **Protecting Cells In A Worksheet**

  - Unlocking Cells
  - Protecting The Worksheet

Automatic Data Validation

Validating Data

Comments and on-screen direction can be used by the person designing the spreadsheet to control data input, ie how the data should be inserted in a cell or whether a cell can be left blank or needs to have data input. If the user then tries to enter data that has not been specified by the spreadsheet designer, the cell will not accept the entry and a warning will appear to suggest how the data should be entered.

Click on the cell that you wish to control input for and select **Data, Validation** from the menu bar.

Click on the **Settings** tab.

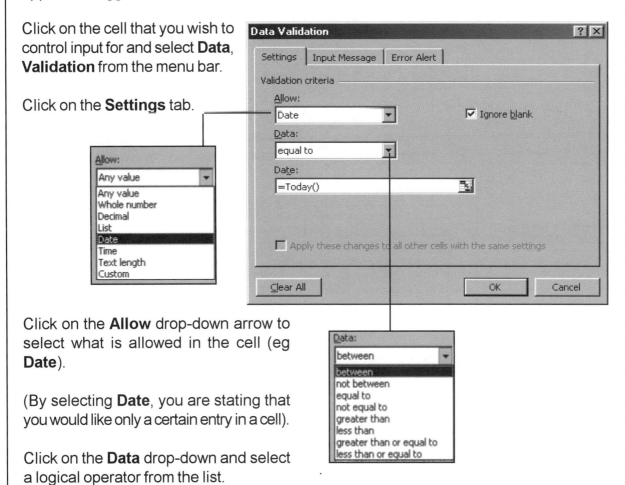

Click on the **Allow** drop-down arrow to select what is allowed in the cell (eg **Date**).

(By selecting **Date**, you are stating that you would like only a certain entry in a cell).

Click on the **Data** drop-down and select a logical operator from the list.

The example above has used **=Today()**, which is a date function used by Excel to ensure today's date is used.

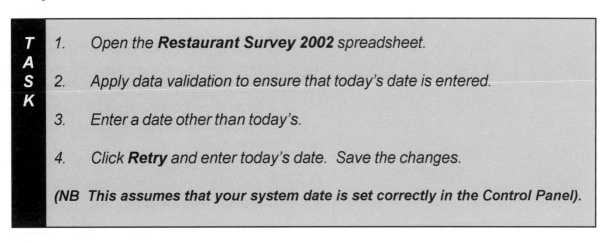

T A S K

1. Open the **Restaurant Survey 2002** spreadsheet.

2. Apply data validation to ensure that today's date is entered.

3. Enter a date other than today's.

4. Click **Retry** and enter today's date. Save the changes.

(NB This assumes that your system date is set correctly in the Control Panel).

Validation Error Messages

To ensure the appropriate data is entered each time a user uses the spreadsheet, input messages and error alerts can be set.

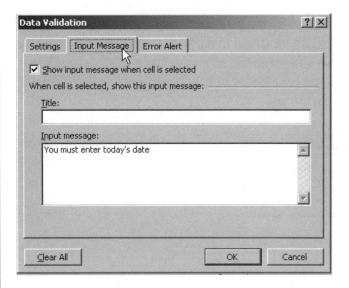

An **input message** will appear when the user moves into that cell on the worksheet. Click on the **Input Message** tab. Ensure there is a tick in the box **Show input message when cell is selected**.

You may give the message a title if required in the **Title** box. However, this can be left blank. Type your input message in the box and click **OK** to apply.

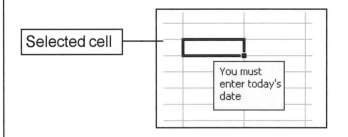

Selected cell

Stop error alert – this type of error alert will not allow invalid data to be entered into the cell. If invalid data is input, a message will appear with a Retry or Cancel button. Retry enables the user to try again and Cancel will restore the previous value to the cell (or leave it blank).

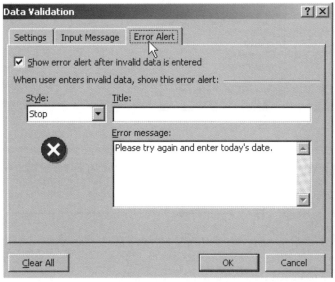

Warning error alert – this type of error alert displays a warning, but gives the user the option to continue. A warning message appears with the text **Continue?** The user can choose **Yes**, **No** or **Cancel**. If the user clicks on **Yes**, then the invalid data will be allowed in the cell.

Information error alert – this type of error alert simply displays information about the cell. The user has the option to click on **OK** or **Cancel**. If they click on **OK**, then invalid data will be allowed in the cell.

For this example, when the cell is selected by a user, the following message will appear.

For this example, if the user enters the wrong date, the following message appears:

To remove validation, click on the cell, choose **Data**, click **Validation** and **Clear All**. Click on **Clear All** in the dialogue box and then **OK**.

T A S K	*Still working within the file restaurant survey:*
	1. *Add an input message and error alert to the previously applied data validation.*
	2. *Click on the cell and view your message.*
	3. *Remove all validation codes (if applied). Remove the inserted date.*

Using IF Functions For Validation

Data validation is useful on its own. However, you can help the person who inputs data further by using the IF function to check cells and provide messages to the user.

Choose **Insert** on the menu bar and click on **Function**. Alternatively, you can press the **Paste Function** button on the Standard toolbar. f_x

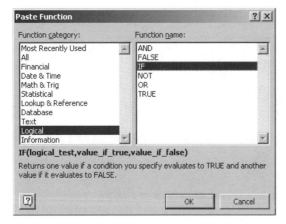

An IF function is a logical function (it can be found in the **Logical** category).

Click on the IF function name in the list on the right and click on **OK**.

The formula palette will be displayed.

An IF function has three parts:

Logical test   a test that you wish it to perform - for example, does a specified cell contain data meeting a specified criteria, eg B1>200?

Value if true   what you want Excel to do if the cell <u>does</u> meet the specified criteria (an IF can return a message or carry out a calculation).

Value if false   what you want Excel to do if the cell <u>does not</u> meet the specified criteria (an IF can return a message or carry out a calculation).

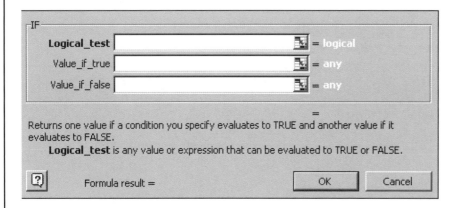

A typical IF function would have the following format:

=IF(test, "result if true", "result if false")

An IF function is also referred to as an IF statement.

In the following example, I want to test whether cell **B2** is blank. If it is, I want a message to appear in cell **C2**. If it isn't, I want a different message to appear in cell **C2**. (The IF statement must be written in cell **C2**).

	A	B	C
1	Survey on local restaurants		
2	by		
3	ID		
4	Date		

The IF statement would look like this:

=IF(B2=0, "Please enter the Researcher's name", "Thank you for entering the Researcher's name")

(The "" indicate that a text message will appear).

The following would appear in the formula palette:

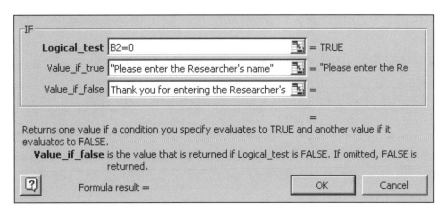

Once the IF statement has been created, the worksheet would look like this:

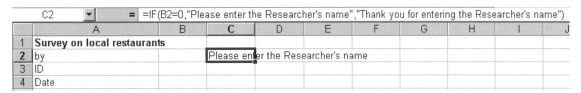

You can use any of the following logical operators when creating an IF statement:

=	equal to
<>	not equal to
<	less than
>	greater than
<=	less than or equal to
>=	greater than or equal to

T A S K

1. *Ensure you are working on the **Restaurant Survey 2002** spreadsheet.*

2. *Enter an IF function in cell **C7**. The IF function is to produce the following result:*

   *If cell **B7** is blank "**Advise availability of discount**".*

   *If cell **B7** is not blank "**Give customer discount vouchers for favourite restaurant**".*

3. *Format the cell so that the statement appears in bold and a larger font size.*

4. *Test the IF statement by typing in your name in cell **B7**. Now delete your name and watch the statement change.*

If you do not want a message to appear, type the speech marks with nothing between ie **" "**. If **0** is to appear, type this between the speech marks, ie **"0"**.

NB Zero values can be hidden on a spreadsheet. Choose **Tools** on the menu bar and click **Options**. Click on the **View** tab and clear the **Zero values** box.

TASK

1. In cell **C14**, create an IF statement that translates as: if the price is more than £50, display the message "**too expensive**"; if not, display the message "**family rates**". Your function should look like:

   =IF(B14>50, "Too Expensive", "Family Rates")

   | Note you should not put the £ sign in the function |

2. Create a data validation formula in the cell to the right of each data entry cell so that, if it is blank, the words "Please enter Name" or "Please enter your ID" appear as necessary.

   Your functions should look like:

   In cell **C2**   **=IF(B2=0,"Please enter name","")**
   In cell **C3**   **=IF(B3=0,"Please enter ID","")**
   In cell **C4**   **=IF(B4=0,"Please enter today's date","")**

3. Save the changes to the spreadsheet.

4. Produce a printout showing the formulae used.

Protecting Cells In A Worksheet

Unlocking Cells

When a worksheet is protected, all the cells on the worksheet are protected, ie a user would not be able to input data into any of the cells. If you wish to be able to enter data into some cells on the worksheet, these need to be 'unlocked' prior to protecting the worksheet.

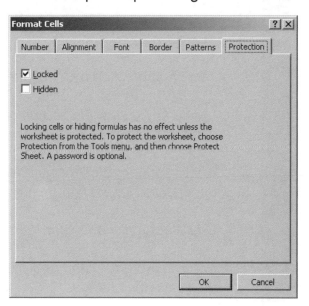

Select the range of cells that you wish to 'unlock' (Remember, you can use the **Ctrl** key on the keyboard to select separate ranges).

Choose **Format** on the menu bar and click on **Cells**. The **Format Cells** dialogue box will open. Click on the **Protection** tab.

Notice that the cells you have selected are **Locked**. Remove the tick from the box to 'unlock' the cells.

Click **OK**.

Protecting The Worksheet

Now you can protect the worksheet. The user will still have access to the cells that have been unlocked.

Choose **Tools** on the menu bar and click on **Protection**, **Protect Sheet.**

You can set a password on sheet protection. This means that the protection cannot be removed without typing in the password. **(You must remember the password that you choose.)**

Click **OK**.

Test out the protection by trying to input data into 'locked' cells. You will receive the following message:

However, you will still be able to enter data into the 'unlocked cells'.

To remove protection, choose **Tools** on the menu bar and click on **Protection**, **Unprotect Sheet** (if you have set a password, you will be prompted to type in the password to unprotect the sheet).

T A S K	1. *Ensure you are working on the **Restaurant survey 2002** workbook.*
	2. *Unlock cells **B2:B21** and protect the worksheet; a password is not required.*
	3. *Test the protection by trying to enter data into various cells.*
	4. *Delete any data within the unlocked area of the spreadsheet. Save the changes.*
	5. *Check your spreadsheet is now protected where the data is constant and unprotected for user data entry.*
	6. *Unprotect your worksheet.*
	7. *Practise protecting and unprotecting different parts of your worksheet and then save the changes.*
	8. *Unlock cells **B2:B21** and protect the worksheet.*
	9. *Save the changes and close the spreadsheet.*

 ©Tektra TEKSS2RP1102

Scenario

You are asked to design a spreadsheet to show how many people each market researcher questioned, how many were sent to their local restaurant, how much each restaurant paid for the visit (a fixed fee of £4.31 was paid) and how much commission each researcher made on the total paid by the restaurant to the company.

1. *Your data input form can be created in a word processing package or by hand. The commission earned is 15% of the total fees paid.*

Market Research January 2002

Name of Researcher	People Questioned	People sent to local restaurant	Price paid by restaurant for each visit
Jane Smith			£4.31
Peter Holloway			
Jennifer Johnson			
Malcolm Writer			
Sharon Ryman			
Joan Fence			
Robert Brewster			
Commission earned	15%		

2. *Produce a design sketch, remembering that there will be sections that are not showing on your data input form. You will need to add a total price paid by restaurant column, as well as copying the researchers' names down to another section of the spreadsheet to enter their commission.*

3. *Label your headings and titles. Show what format each cell should be, ie currency, number, percentage, text. Decide on the column widths.*

4. *Show what information is constant input data, variable input data and output data. Show what formulas and functions you would use to achieve your output data.*

5. *Finally, do some calculations to test your formulae using sample figures for people sent to local restaurant.*

6. *At the moment do not create your spreadsheet in Excel. You will use the information to create the spreadsheet in unit 5.*

7. *Close any open documents.*

The sidebar reads vertically: **CONSOLIDATION EXERCISE**

On completion of this unit, you will have learnt about and practised the following:

- **Naming Cells And Ranges**

  - Naming Cells And Ranges
  - Inserting And Deleting Rows And Columns
  - Inserting Formulae Using Named Cells

- **Copying Options**

  - Copying Formulae To Other Cells
  - AutoFill And Other Options

- **Relative And Absolute References**

- **Freezing And Splitting Spreadsheets**

- **Hiding Columns And Rows**

  - Hiding A Row Or Column
  - Unhiding A Row Or Column

Naming Cells And Ranges

It is possible to assign names to cells and ranges in order to make the worksheet easier to navigate. Names can also reduce errors in formulae. By using the names in formulae, the calculation is easier to recognise, ie **=Price*Quantity** is easier than =**A4*B4**.

T A S K

Use the design of the spreadsheet created in the Consolidation Exercise in the previous unit to carry out this task.

1. *Type in the data from your Data Input Form. It should look similar to that below. Add the figures for People Questioned and People Referred. Set the column widths, fonts and formats from your sketch.*

2. *Format the titles (row 1) so that the cells 'wrap text'.*

	A	B	C	D	E	F	G	H
1	Name of Researcher	People Questioned	People sent to local restaurant	Price paid by restaurant	Total price paid by restaurant			
2	Jane Smith	20	11	£4.31				
3	Peter Holloway	34	24	£4.31				
4	Jennifer Johnson	45	28	£4.31			Commission earned	15%
5	Malcolm Writer	19	15	£4.31				
6	Sharon Ryman	48	43	£4.31				
7	Joan Fence	34	23	£4.31				
8	Robert Brewster	20	3	£4.31				
9								

3. *Save the spreadsheet as **Research**.*

T A S K

1. *In cell **H4**, type **0.15**, then format the cell to percentage to give 15%.*

2. *Save the document as **Research**.*

   NB   If you type 15, and then format the cell to percentage, you will get 1500%, which would be an incorrect amount.

Naming Cells And Ranges

To give a cell or a range of cells a defined name, first select the cell or cells.

Click **Insert**, **Name** and select **Define** from the menu bar.

Type a name for your selected cell(s)

Cell names are added here. Spaces and most symbols are not accepted.

To separate words, use the 'underscore' key on the keyboard.

Other cell names are shown here.

Click **OK** to apply the name.

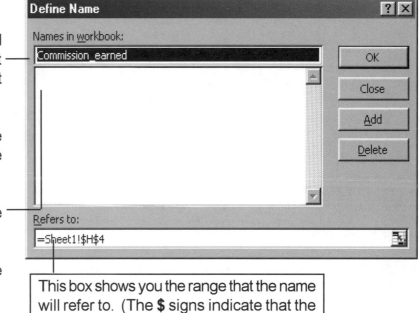

This box shows you the range that the name will refer to. (The **$** signs indicate that the named range is absolute).

Alternatively, you can use the **Name Box** at the left end of the Formula bar to name ranges on the worksheet.

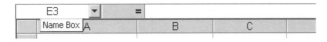

Click on the cell or range of cells that you wish to name, click in the Name Box and type a name for the selected cell(s).

You must press Enter after typing the name.

Once you have named cells and ranges on the worksheet, you can use the **Name** drop-down list to navigate to those named cell(s) on the worksheet.

Click on the name in the list to move to that part of the worksheet.

To remove a defined name, choose **Insert** on the menu bar and click **Names**, **Define**.

Select the name you wish to delete in the list and click on **Delete**.

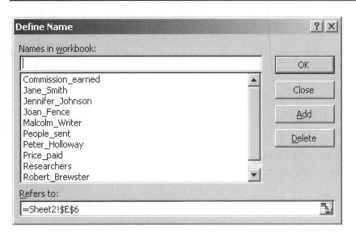

T
A
S
K

1. Using the **Research** spreadsheet.

2. Format cells **D2:D8** to currency, 2 decimal places.

3. Name cell **H4** as **Commission_earned**.

4. Name the cell ranges that contain data for:

   People Questioned
   People sent to local restaurant
   Price paid by restaurant
   Total price paid by restaurant

5. Save the changes.

Inserting And Deleting Rows And Columns

Additional rows and columns can be inserted onto a worksheet.

Columns are inserted to the left of the current column. **Rows** are inserted above the current row.

To insert a column, select the column to the right of where the new column is to be inserted and choose **Insert** on the menu bar. Click **Columns**.

To insert a row, select the row below where the new row is to be inserted and choose **Insert** on the menu bar. Click **Rows**.

If you wish to insert more than one row or column at a time, select the number of rows or columns you wish to insert.

For example, to insert four rows above row 3, select rows 3, 4, 5 and 6. When you choose **Insert, Rows**, four rows will be inserted above the selected rows. Rows 3 to 6 will then be moved on to become 7,8,9 and 10.

To insert four columns to the left of column B, select columns B, C, D and E. When you choose **Insert, Columns**, four columns will be inserted to the left of the selected columns.

To delete rows or columns, select the row(s) or column(s) that you wish to delete and choose **Edit** on the menu bar. Click **Delete**.

Redefining Named Cell Ranges

When you insert rows or columns, named cells will update automatically. However, you may need to redefine named ranges. Click **Insert**, **Name**, **Define** from the menu bar to display the **Define Name** dialogue box.

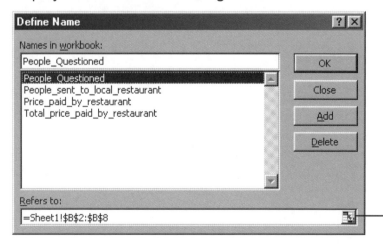

Select the named range in the list. The cell references will appear in the **Refers to** box.

Click into the **Refers to** box and edit the range or click on the red arrow button to collapse the dialogue box. Select the new cell range. Click on the red arrow button to expand the dialogue box and click **Add** to update the references.

Inserting Formulae Using Named Cells

To total the Total price paid by restaurant, your formula would be People sent to local restaurant multiplied by Price paid by restaurant (ie £4.31). To use the named ranges in the formula, start your formula (=) and then choose **Insert** on the menu bar and click **Name**, **Paste**.

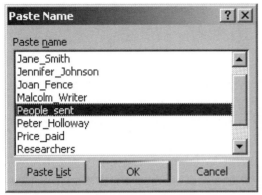

Select the named range you wish to use and click on **OK**.

Type your mathematical operator (in this case *) and then choose **Insert**, **Name**, **Paste** again to select the next named range.

Your formula would look like this:

=People_sent*Price_paid

T A S K	1.	*Ensure you are working on the **Research** spreadsheet.*
	2.	*Add the following names to your worksheet:*

> Peter Piper questioned 25 people, 22 were sent to the local restaurant. Janet Gibson questioned 55 people and 48 were sent to the local restaurant. Same 'Price paid by restaurant' as others.

3. *Redefine the ranges to include extra names.*

4. *Using the above method, insert formulas into column E to arrive at a Total Price.*

5. *Save the changes.*

Copying Options

Copying Formulae To Other Cells

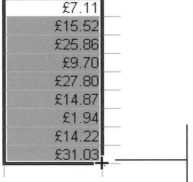

Click on the cell that contains the formula you wish to copy. In the bottom corner of the cell there is a small black square.

Point to the black square with the mouse. A black cross appears. This is the copy handle. Drag this handle down or across through the cells you want to copy the formula into.

When you release the mouse button, the formulae is copied into the selected cells. The cell references have adjusted accordingly to the row or column they have been copied into.

AutoFill And Other Options

The black cross that appears at the bottom of a cell or range of cells has two uses – it can be used to copy formulas into other cells, as described above.

It can also be used to "fill" series. For example, if you type Monday in a cell and then use the fill handle to drag down or across into other cells, Tuesday, Wednesday, Thursday, etc, will appear in the consecutive cells. This fill handle can be used for days of the week, months of the year and dates (Excel must recognise the first cell as a date before it will use the calendar).

You can also use the fill handle to fill in data or date intervals, but you will need to type in the first two entries in the series. For example, if you type **5** in a cell and **10** in the next cell, then select both of these cells, you can use the fill handle to continue the series – 15, 20, 25, etc. If you type two dates in consecutive cells and select them both, you can use the fill handle to continue the series in the same pattern.

T A S K		
	1.	*Ensure you are working on the **Research** spreadsheet.*
	2.	*Copy cells **A1:H22** to Sheet 2.*
	3.	*Rename the sheets as below, by double-clicking on the sheet tab, typing in the new name and pressing **Enter** on the keyboard to confirm.*

▶ ▶| \ **Copy with named cells** ⟋ Copy with formulas ⟋

T A S K

4.   Resize the column widths as necessary.

5.   Using the **Copy with formulas** sheet, delete all the defined names.

   *(Once you have done this, your Total price column will show an error in each cell, **#NAME?**. This is because you have a formula using named references but these no longer exist. Delete all the error messages in the column).*

6.   Create the numerical formula, ie **=C2*D2**, and copy down.

7.   Show the formula and ensure all formulae relate to the appropriate row number.

8.   Save the changes.

Relative And Absolute References

A relative reference allows you to copy the formula to a new cell. The cell reference will change according to the new row or column it is being copied to.

An absolute reference, ie Commission earned, always refers to a particular cell address and will continue to do so even if the formula is moved to a new location. Absolute cell references can be identified by the presence of a dollar sign ($) before the column letter and row number of the address, ie **$D$10**.

For example, in the spreadsheet to the right, each person has achieved a sub-total. However they will each receive a bonus of 100 pounds. By making cell **G13** an absolute cell reference, the formula can be copied down, but will always refer to cell **G13**.

	F	G	H
7	**Name**	**Sub-Total**	**Total**
8			
9	Ann	56	=G9+$G$13
10	John	56	=G10+$G$13
11	Andrew	67	=G11+$G$13
12			
13	**Bonus**	100	

To make a cell reference absolute in a formula, insert the dollar signs manually or press **F4** on the keyboard.

T A S K

1. Ensure you are working on the **Copy with formulas** sheet within the **Research** spreadsheet.

2. Copy cells **A1** to **A10** into cell **A13** etc.

3. In cell **B14**, insert the formula to calculate the commission earned by **Jane Smith** (Total Price * 15% ie **E2*$H$4**).

4. Copy the formula down to the other cells. Notice how each row reference changes relative to the researcher but the reference to the cell containing the commission earned information remains the same, as this cell reference is absolute.

5. Save the changes.

Freezing And Splitting Spreadsheets

Imagine a large spreadsheet spanning many columns and rows. You may have to scroll through the worksheet to add, delete, modify or view information. As you scroll down or across the worksheet the headings scroll off the screen. If you cannot see the row or column headings, the data can be confusing.

You can **freeze** columns and rows on the worksheet so that they do not scroll off the screen as you navigate around the worksheet. This enables you to view separate areas of the worksheet at the same time. **Panes** are the columns and rows that remain in place, or freeze, whilst the rest of the worksheet scrolls.

Freezing panes may not be sufficient in a very large worksheet so you can also split the worksheet into as many as four panes at once and then move in between each one easily.

For example, in the Sales spreadsheet, the names of the Sales Reps are not visible when scrolling down to view the rest of the data.

Specify which sections are to be frozen by clicking into a cell. Any columns to the left, or rows above the active cell will be frozen.

Click **Window**, **Freeze Panes** from the menu bar.

Lines will appear horizontally and vertically across the spreadsheet to divide it into four sections.

You can now scroll down or across the worksheet and the data in the frozen panes does not move. To unfreeze panes click **Window**, **Unfreeze Panes** from the menu bar.

There are two ways to **split the window**.

At the top of the vertical scroll bar and at the right end of the horizontal scroll bar, there is a grey bar. Click on this bar and drag it onto the screen. A split appears where you drop the bar down.

Vertical scroll bar

Horizontal scroll bar

Alternatively, you can choose **Window**, **Split** and this will split your window into four **panes.**

To remove the splits, either move the mouse over each split until the pointer changes to a double-headed arrow, then double-click or choose **Window**, **Remove Split**.

T A S K

1. Open the spreadsheet called **Sales**.

2. You cannot see the names of the sales representatives as you move down the spreadsheet. Freeze the panes to make them visible at all times.

Hiding Columns And Rows

Your spreadsheet may contain information that you do not want other users to see. To hide information that is confidential or that you do not want to make available to other users, columns and rows can be hidden from view. Hidden columns or rows are not printed.

Hiding A Row Or Column

Select the row or column that you wish to hide and choose **Format** on the menu bar. Click on **Column** or **Row** and choose **Hide**.

Unhiding A Row Or Column

To unhide a hidden row or column, select the rows or columns on either side of the hidden row or column. Choose **Format** on the menu bar. Click on **Column** or **Row** and choose **Unhide**.

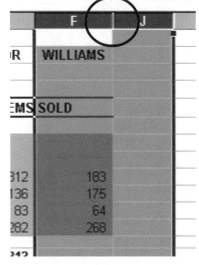

> In this example columns **G**, **H** and **I** have been hidden.
>
> To unhide them, select columns **F** and **J** and choose **Format**, **Column**, **Unhide**.

You cannot hide data if a spreadsheet is protected. Unprotect the sheet, hide your data and then protect it again.

TASK

1. Open the spreadsheet called *Sales*.

2. Hide column *I*.

3. Protect the worksheet.

4. Print a copy in portrait orientation.

5. Unhide column *I* (you will have to unprotect the worksheet to do this).

6. Print the worksheet.

7. Save the changes.

8. Close the spreadsheet.

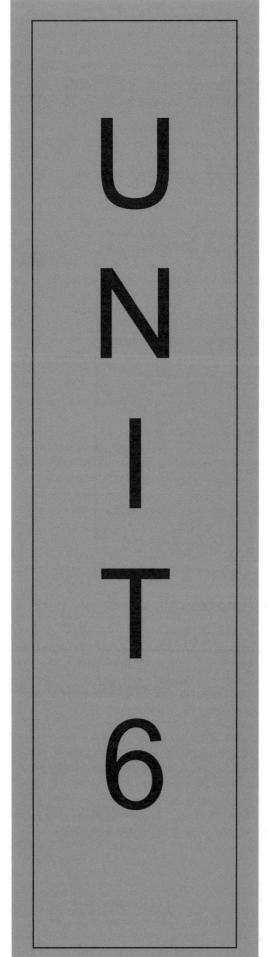

On completion of this unit, you will have learnt about and practised the following:

- **Using Functions**

  - The Sum Function
  - The Average Function
  - The Maximum And Minimum Functions
  - The Count Function
  - The Date Function
  - Paste Special
  - The Round Function
  - Linking Worksheets/ Workbooks
  - Using Paste Link

- **Working With Worksheets**

  - Inserting Worksheets Into Existing Workbooks
  - Deleting Worksheets
  - Renaming Worksheets
  - Moving Or Copying Worksheets
  - Viewing Multiple Worksheets
  - Viewing Multiple Workbooks

Using Functions

Functions are predefined formulae that enable you to create complex calculations easily. Like formula, functions always begin with the **=** sign and you can enter them manually or insert a function, choose **Insert** on the menu bar and click on **Function**. Alternatively, press the **Paste Function** button on the Standard toolbar.

The Sum Function

The SUM function is a common function used in Excel as it can quickly add a range of cells and return the result. A fast way of inserting this function is to use the **AutoSum** button on the Standard toolbar.

Click in the cell where you want the result to appear first.

Click on the **AutoSum** button.   Σ

A moving border will appear around the row or column that AutoSum predicts you wish to add. If the prediction is correct, press **Enter** and the result will be displayed.

T A S K

1. *Open the spreadsheet called **Research**, select the **Copy with formulas** sheet.*

2. *Enter a function to total (sum) the researchers' commission earned in cell **B24**.*

3. *Add the following labels (headings) in the specified cells and resize as necessary:*

   A24 - Total
   B13 - Commission Earned
   C13 - Average
   D13 - Maximum
   E13 - Minimum

4. *Save the changes.*

The Average Function

The average function is used to calculate the average of a given number of values in a range of cells. To use a function, click in the cell where the result (calculation) is required and click on the **Paste Function** button. f_x

This will display the **Paste Function** dialogue box:

Functions are grouped into categories and there are many available.

When a category is selected on the left, the functions in that category are displayed on the right.

If you are unsure of which function to use, click to select it and read the description in the lower part of the dialogue box.

Click **OK** to select one.

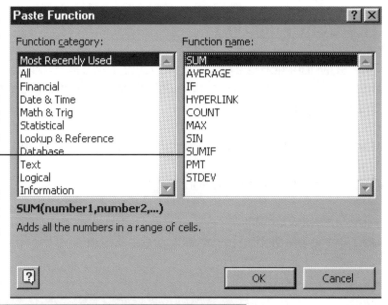

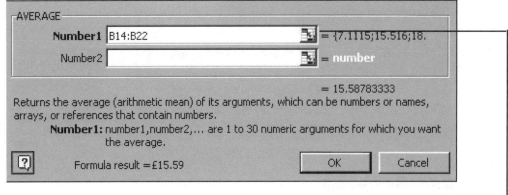

When a function has been selected (**AVERAGE** in this example), the **formula palette** will appear. Click on the red arrow button to temporarily collapse the palette and select the cells on the worksheet that you wish to include in the function. Click on the red arrow button again to expand the formula palette and click on **OK**. Alternatively, you can type the cell range into the **Number1** box and click on **OK**.

Alternatively functions can be typed in manually if you know the function name (eg **=SUM**, **=AVERAGE**).

=average(B14:B22)

T	1.	*Ensure you are working on the **Copy with formulas** sheet within the **Research** spreadsheet.*
A		
S		
K	2.	*Insert a function into cell **C24** to find the average commission earned. Save the changes.*

The Maximum And Minimum Functions

The maximum (**MAX**) function will calculate the highest value in a given range of cells.

To use the maximum function, either use the **Paste Function** button and select it from the list, then select the range on the worksheet, or

type in: | =max(range of cells) |

To minimise the dialogue book, click the red arrow on the top box.

The minimum (**MIN**) function will calculate the lowest value in a given range of cells.

To use the minimum function, either use the **Paste Function** button and select it from the list, then select the range on the worksheet, or

type in: | =min(range of cells) |

Once again, to minimise the dialogue book, click the red arrow on the top box.

T A S K

1. *Insert a function into cell **D24** to find the maximum commission earned.*

2. *Insert a function into cell **E24** to find the minimum commission earned.*

3. *Save the changes.*

4. *View the formulae.*

5. *Print a copy of the spreadsheet showing the formula. Ensure all columns are visible and fit on one page.*

6. *Hide the formulae again.*

The Count Function

The **COUNT** function is used to count a number of specified cells in a worksheet. Although you can easily see that you have 9 researchers, if your spreadsheet had hundreds of names and you needed to know exactly how many people were involved, you could use the COUNT functions.

The four different types of COUNT functions are:

1. COUNT   -   Counts cells containing only numerical data.

2. COUNTA   -   Counts cells containing any type of data.

3. COUNTBLANK -   Counts only cells that are blank.

4. COUNTIF   -   Counts only cells that match a specified criteria.

To use the **COUNT** function, either select it using the **Paste Function** button and then select the range on the worksheet, or

type in: | =COUNTA(range of cells) |

TASK

1. *Add a label in cell **A29** and type:* **Count**

2. *Insert a function in **B29** to total the number of researchers.*

3. *Save the worksheet and close.*

The Date Function

If you enter dates into a spreadsheet and use date formatting, you can perform date calculations. For example, you can calculate the number of days an invoice has been outstanding or the number of days between today and your birthday. When you enter a date in any of the commonly used date formats, Excel sees the entry as a date function and converts it to a date serial number (you can only see this number if you change the format of the date cell to **General**). For example, the serial date of 1 January, 1900 is 1, the serial date of 2 January, 1900 is 2, the serial date of 1 January 2002 is 37257.

To calculate the number of days between dates the following method can be used:

1. Enter each date into individual cells ie today's date in cell **D4** and my birthday date in cell **E4**.
2. Format the cell containing the formula to general.
3. Enter a formula to subtract one date series from another, ie = **E4-D4**.
4. Format the dates to show any of the commonly used date formats.

Functions such as **=TODAY()** and **=NOW()** will display today's date or today's date and the time.

T A S K

1. *Open a blank spreadsheet and perform some date calculations such as:*

    *   *How many days between now and Christmas?*
    *   *How many days between your birthday and today?*

2. *Insert today's date using your preferred method in cell **B3**. In the adjacent cell, type **=B3+30**. This will give you the date in 30 days' time.*

3. *Close the spreadsheet, do not save the changes.*

Paste Special

When you copy and paste a cell it will carry with it all cell contents, including the formula and the result. It is possible to paste only values, formulas, comments or cell formats by using **Paste Special**.

Instead of pasting entire cell contents, you can paste specified contents from the cells. For example, you can paste the resulting value of a formula without pasting the formula itself.

1. Select the cell(s) to copy and click **Copy**.
2. Select cell(s) to copy to.
3. Click **Edit**, **Paste Special** from the menu bar to display the **Paste Special** dialogue box.

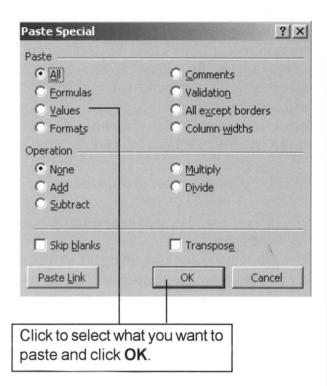

Click to select what you want to paste and click **OK**.

The **Paste** section of the **Paste Special** dialogue box is used to indicate which parts of a copied cell you wish to paste, eg values only. In this case, the resulting value of a cell would be pasted, however the formula behind the calculation would not be pasted.

For example:

The values only have been pasted from cells **H9:H11** to cells **J9:J11**.

The format and formula from the original cells was not required.

The result is the value only appearing in column **J**. When one of the cells is selected, the Formula bar will show the value (not the formula, as it is no longer present).

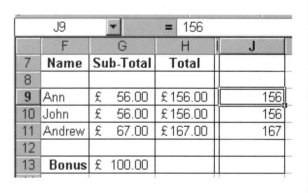

If a normal Copy and Paste had been used the formula itself would have been pasted. Because of relative cell referencing, the formula would change to calculate the new column to the left (**I**) * **$G$13** (this cell reference does not change as it is absolute). This will result in an incorrect figure.

T A S K		
	1.	Open the spreadsheet called **Research**, click on **Copy with formulas** sheet.
	2.	Apply an outline border to cells **A1:E1** and copy the formats of this range to a blank sheet (cell **A1**).
	3.	Copy all headings to the same location using the 'values' option from paste special and format the column widths to accommodate the headings.
	4.	Copy the cells **A2:D10** into the new sheet.
	5.	Delete columns **B**, **C** and **D**.
	6.	Copy the **values** only from the Total price paid by restaurant column into the new sheet.
	7.	Give the new sheet a suitable name. Save the changes.

The Round Function

If you display figures to only one or two decimal places, then rounding 'errors' can occur. When you decrease the number of decimal places, Excel will always round up the figure. For example, the figure 2.87 will display as 2.9 if you only have one decimal place and 3 if you have no decimal places. When carrying out calculations containing currency (pounds and pence), this can make a difference to the result. Excel will change the appearance of your data in the cell, but not the actual value. The 'real value' is used in calculations. The **Round** function can be used to prevent errors occurring when calculations are carried out on currency values.

T A S K		
	1.	View the **Copy with formulas** sheet within the **Research** workbook.
	2.	Format the Commission earned cells (**B14-22**) to **General.**
		(This will display the real values made, by calculating the percentage of commission earned.) Make a note of these on a spare piece of paper.
	3.	Format the cells back to Currency.

If you are working with currency, you will probably want to view the figures to 2 decimal places. This may result in a rounding 'error'. The rounding error is the difference between the real value and the rounded value. For example, if Jane Smith's commission is rounded, there will be a rounding error of £0.0015. This is calculated by deducting the rounded value from the real value, ie:

=7.1115-7.11

=£0.0015

Although this does not appear very much, it would add up if Jane had interviewed 1000 people.

To use the **Round** function, you can type the function in manually, or use the **Paste Function** button on the Standard toolbar.

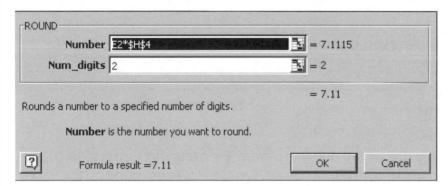

The **ROUND** function needs two bits of information: the number (or calculation) that you wish to round and the number of decimal places you want to round it to.

In the case of the commission calculation, the formula that needs to be rounded is **E2*$H$4** and the number of decimal places is 2.

If you typed this formula manually it would look like this:

=ROUND(E2*$H$4, 2)

T A S K

1. In cell **B14**, edit the function to appear as follows:

   =ROUND(E2*$H$4,2)

   The ,2 tells Excel to round to 2 decimal places.

2. Copy the function to the remaining cells.

3. Change the cell formats to general, compare with the noted amounts.

4. Change the format back to Currency.

5. Save the spreadsheet.

6. Close the spreadsheet.

Linking Worksheets/Workbooks

Linking is used to produce a result in a cell on one sheet which is related to another cell, either on a different worksheet or in a different workbook.

Linking Worksheets

Imagine your workbook contains six worksheets, each representing a month of the year. Each sheet shows monthly expenses which, when added, will produce a Total Expenses figure for the month. The Total Expenses figure needs to be shown on a summary sheet rather than on monthly sheets. By linking the two sheets together (ie by creating a formula), the summary sheet will always be showing the latest figures (being provided by the other sheets in the workbook).

1. Click in the cell where you wish the result of the linked formula to appear (ie a cell on the summary sheet.

2. Type = to begin the formula, use AutoSum or type the function you wish to use in this example, it would be =SUM).

3. Select the cell or range of cells that you need to reference for the formula. This may mean navigating to another worksheet. (Click with the mouse on the sheet you need to move to and then select the cell or range of cells on that sheet that you need to reference.) The formula bar will show the route you have navigated (ie sheet name and cell reference).

4. In the case of a SUM function, you can now press **Return** to return to the summary sheet with your result. However, if you are building a formula that includes more than one cell reference, type the mathematical operator and then repeat step 3 to navigate to the next cell reference required.

NB **Always press Return (Enter) when you have finished building your formula to return to the original cell.**

Linking Workbooks

Imagine your workbook contains six worksheets, each representing a month of the year. Each sheet shows monthly expenses which, when added, will produce a Total Expenses figure for the month. The Total Expenses figure needs to be shown on a summary sheet which is in another workbook. By linking the two workbooks together (ie by creating a formula), the summary sheet will always be showing the latest figures (being provided by the other workbook).

You will find it easier to create the formula if both workbooks are open and tiled on the screen so that you can see them side by side. (Choose **Window** on the menu bar and click **Arrange**. Choose **Tiled**.)

1.   Click in the cell where you wish the result of the linked formula to appear (ie a cell on the summary sheet).

2.   Type **=** to begin the formula, use AutoSum or type the function you wish to use (in this example, it would be **=SUM**).

3.   Select the cell or range of cells that you need to reference for the formula. This may mean navigating to the other workbook. (Click with the mouse in the other workbook, click on the sheet you require and then select the cell or range of cells on that sheet that you need to reference.) The formula bar will show the route you have navigated, ie file name, sheet name and cell reference.

4.   In the case of a **SUM** function, you can now press **Return** to return to the summary workbook with your result. However, if you are building a formula that includes more than one cell reference, type the mathematical operator and then repeat step 3 to navigate to the next cell reference required.

NB   Always press Return (Enter) when you have finished building your formula to return to the original cell.

	A	B
1		**Expenses Sur**
2	Month	Value
3	January	='[Monthly Expenses.xls]January'!$C$12
4	February	='[Monthly Expenses.xls]February'!$C$12
5	March	='[Monthly Expenses.xls]March'!$C$12
6	April	='[Monthly Expenses.xls]April'!$C$12
7	May	='[Monthly Expenses.xls]May'!$C$12
8	June	='[Monthly Expenses.xls]June'!$C$12

In this example, the formula is stating that the cell is to equal cell reference **C12** in the January Worksheet of the Monthly Expense Workbook.

T
A
S
K

1. Open the spreadsheet called **Research**.

2. Select the cell range **A13:A22** (Names of Researchers) and copy this range onto a new sheet (**A1**).

3. In cell **B1** of the new sheet, type the heading **Commission Earned**.

4. Create a calculation to calculate the commission earned, using the information on the **Copy with formulas** sheet (don't worry about rounding).

5. Save the spreadsheet.

6. Select the cell range **A13:A22** (Names of Researchers) and copy this range into a new workbook (**A1**).

7. In cell **B1** of the new workbook, type the heading **Commission Earned**.

8. Create a calculation to calculate the commission earned, using the information in the **Research** workbook, **Copy with formulas** sheet.

9. Print a copy of the new workbook, showing the formulas. Save the workbook as **Linked** to you floppy disk.

10. Close all open workbooks.

Using Paste Link

The other way to link two or more worksheets or workbooks together is by using **Paste Link**. Select the cell or range of cells that you wish to link and copy in the normal way. Move to the destination worksheet or workbook and choose **Edit** on the menu bar. Click on **Paste Special** and click the **Paste Link** button.

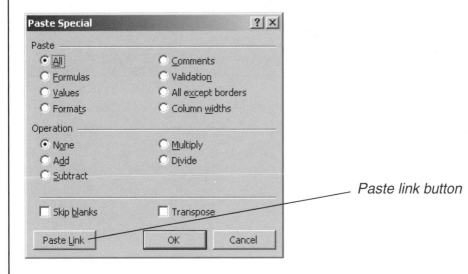

Paste link button

Excel automatically creates a formula that links the two sets of cells together.

Working With Worksheets

Inserting Worksheets Into Existing Workbooks

When you are working with large amounts of data, it may be necessary to split the information onto separate worksheets. By default, every new workbook already has three worksheets that you can use. You can change this default in **Tools**, **Options** or you can insert another worksheet when required.

Click **Insert**, **Worksheet** from the menu bar.

Alternatively, you can right-click on the **Sheet** tab and choose **Insert** from the shortcut menu. A new worksheet will be inserted in front of the current worksheet.

To move an inserted worksheet, point to the **Sheet** tab with the mouse, click, hold and drag the sheet to a new location.

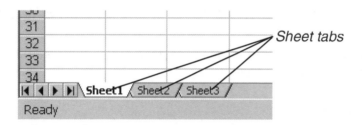

Sheet tabs

T **A** **S** **K**	1. Open **Sales** spreadsheet.
	2. Unprotect the worksheet (if necessary).
	3. Insert a new worksheet.
	4. Reposition the new worksheet to appear to the right of the **Sales** worksheet.
	5. Save and close the workbook.

Deleting Worksheets

The quickest way to delete a sheet is to right-click on the sheet tab and the following shortcut menu will appear:

Click on **Delete** and the following message will appear to warn you before you delete the sheet:

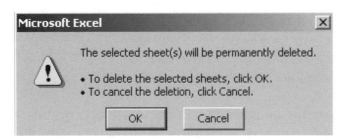

(If you would rather use the menu bar, click on the sheet you wish to delete and choose **Edit** on the menu bar. Click on **Delete Sheet.**)

Renaming Worksheets

To rename a worksheet, right-click on the sheet tab and choose **Rename** from the shortcut menu. The current name is selected and you can over-type the new name.

Moving or Copying Worksheets

Right-click on the sheet tab and choose **Move** or **Copy** from the shortcut menu.

Select the sheet that you wish to move this sheet before.

If you wish to create a copy of the sheet, check the **Create a copy** box.

Click **OK**.

Viewing Multiple Worksheets

If you have a workbook containing several sheets but you wish to view the sheets side by side on the screen at the same time, you can create new windows.

Open the workbook that you wish to view. The title bar shows the name of the workbook. Choose **Window**, **New Window** from the menu bar. The title bar of the workbook will now have **:2** after the file name. To create another window, choose **New Window** again. The title bar will now have **:3**. Repeat this procedure for as many windows as you want.

You can now switch between the windows by choosing the appropriate window in the **Window** menu. Alternatively, if you wish to view the windows side by side, choose **Window** on the menu bar and click **Arrange**. Choose **Tiled**. Once you have tiled the windows on the screen, you can look at a different sheet in each of the windows.

Viewing Multiple Workbooks

Open all the workbooks that you wish to view. (Each workbook opens into its own 'window'). You can switch between the windows by choosing the appropriate workbook in the **Window** menu. Alternatively, if you wish to view the windows together on the screen, choose **Window** on the menu bar and click **Arrange**.

Tiled	Tiled on the screen – across then down (depending on the number of workbooks)
Horizontal	One above the other
Vertical	Side by side then underneath (depending on the number of workbooks)
Cascade	Overlapping and cascading down the screen

You can also see each of your workbooks on the Taskbar along the bottom of the screen. You can simply click on the workbook you wish to switch to in the Taskbar.

If you open more than one workbook and they don't appear in the Taskbar, choose **Tools** on the menu bar and click **Options**. Click on the **View** tab and click the **Windows in Taskbar** box. Click **OK**.

T A S K

1. *Open the spreadsheets called **Sales**, **Income and Expenditure** and **Research**. The names of the open spreadsheets appear in the Taskbar at the bottom of the screen.* SALES.xls   income and expe...

2. *Switch between the workbooks by clicking on the name in the Taskbar or choose **Window** from the menu bar and click on the file you wish to switch to.*

3. *Arrange the spreadsheets, using the different Arrange options.*

4. *Close the active workbooks.*

C O N S O L I D A T I O N   E X E R C I S E

1. *Start a new workbook.*

2. *Ensure the workbook contains 6 worksheets (insert sheets if necessary).*

3. *Rename the worksheets to* **January**, **February**, **March**, **April**, **May** *and* **June**.

4. *Enter the following data into the January worksheet:*

	A	B	C
1	**Expenses**		
2	**Expense**	**Date**	**Value**
3	Gas	04-Jan	£20.00
4	Electricity	06-Jan	£40.00
5	Water	08-Jan	£15.00
6	Rent	15-Jan	£85.00
7	Council Tax	16-Jan	£70.00
8	Telephone	18-Jan	£60.00
9	Mobile Phone	25-Jan	£20.00
10	Insurance	04-Jan	£12.00
11			
12	Total c/f		£322.00

5. *Merge and centre the cells containing the title. Format to Arial size 24pt and bold.*

6. *The labels in cells* **A2:C2** *are to be formatted to Arial, size 16pt.*

7. *Format the Value column to currency with 2 decimal places.*

8. *Enter a function to total the Value column in cell* **C12**.

9. *Copy the data to all remaining 5 sheets, ensuring the data is positioned in cell* **A1** *when copied.*

10. *Save as* **Monthly Expenses** *and print the* **June** *worksheet.*

11. *Delete the contents of column* **B** *on the February worksheet. Enter the following formula in cell* **B3** *of the February worksheet to make the date calculate 1 month from January (gas is always 4th of the month):*

    =January!B3+31 (ie 31 days in January).

12. *Copy this formula to all remaining cells in the column.*

13. *Repeat this procedure for the remaining months (remember to update and check all formulae, taking into account the number of days in each month).*

	A	B	C
1	**Expenses Summary**		
2	Month	Value	Cumulative Value
3	January		
4	February		
5	March		
6	April		
7	May		
8	June		
9			
10			

14. *Start a new workbook and enter the data shown here. Use similar font sizes etc to those above.*

15. *Save the workbook as* **Summary**.

CONSOLIDATION EXERCISE

16. *Print the workbook.*

17. *Format the Cumulative Value column to Accounting, 2 decimal places.*

18. *Enter a formula in cell **B3** to refer to the **total c/f** figure on the January sheet of the Monthly Expenses workbook.*

    *ie cell **B3** of the Expenses Summary will require the figure from cell **C12** in the January worksheet of the Monthly Expenses workbook.*

19. *Repeat this procedure for each month on the Summary spreadsheet and calculate the cumulative value in column **C**. The first formula will be =B3 in cell **C3**.*

    The remaining formula should add the previous total to the new total etc.

20. *Print the Summary worksheet in Normal view and again showing the formula used. Ensure all cells are fully visible in both views.*

21. *Figures for the Council Tax and Rent have risen from the month of April:*

    Rent - 95.00
    Council Tax - 78.00

    *Update the **Monthly expenses** workbook figures for April, May and June to accommodate this change.*

22. *View the Summary spreadsheet and ensure the figures have been updated.*

23. *Print the spreadsheet in normal view.*

24. *Save the changes to both workbooks.*

25. *Close both workbooks.*

	A	B	C
1	**Expenses Summary**		
2	Month	Value	Cumulative Value
3	January	£322.00	£ 322.00
4	February	£322.00	£ 644.00
5	March	£322.00	£ 966.00
6	April	£340.00	£ 1,306.00
7	May	£340.00	£ 1,646.00
8	June	£340.00	**£ 1,986.00**
9			
10			

UNIT 7

On completion of this unit, you will have learnt about and practised the following:

- **Charts And Graphs**

  - Planning A Chart
  - Creating A Chart
  - Moving And Resizing Charts
  - Editing A Chart
  - Changing The Chart Type
  - Using Paste Special With Charts And Graphs
  - Printing The Chart
  - Formatting Charts

- **Working With Objects**

  - Importing Objects Into A Spreadsheet
  - Inserting An Object Into A Spreadsheet

Charts And Graphs

Charts and graphs are a visual representation of your data. They are visually appealing and make it easy for users to see comparisons, patterns and trends in data. For instance, rather than having to analyse several columns of figures on a worksheet, you could see immediately which researchers were meeting their targets, costs incurred for each month etc.

A selection of the most commonly used charts are:

Bar

Compares values at a given point in time or across categories. Horizontal format.

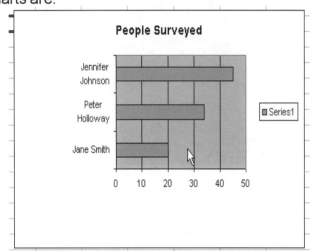

Column

Same as bar but in a vertical format.

Pie

Shows the data as a percentage of the whole. Can have slices pulled away or exploded.

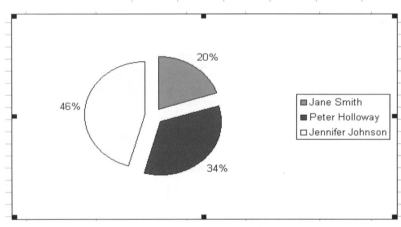

Line

Compares trends over even time intervals.

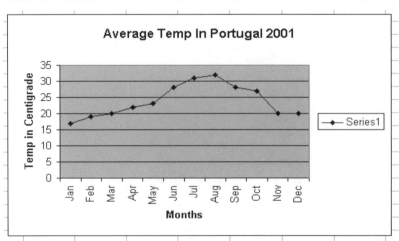

Scatter charts compare trends over uneven time or measured intervals, ie predicted temperature to actual temperature.

Planning A Chart

Before creating a chart, you should determine the purpose of the chart and what visual outcome you require.

You need to decide which type of chart is most appropriate to use and then identify the data that will best illustrate the required outcome.

Creating A Chart

To create a chart, first select the cells required (use the **Ctrl** key to select seperate ranges on the worksheet).

Click **Insert**, **Chart** from the menu bar or click the **Chart Wizard** button on the Standard toolbar. This will display the Chart Wizard which is a series of steps to help create your chart.

Step 1

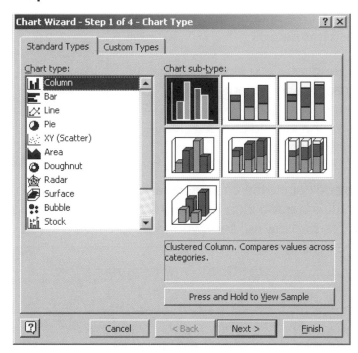

In Step 1, select the **Chart type** you require from the list on the left. A selection of **Chart sub-types** will appear on the right. Select one.

Click **Next** to move on to Step 2.

Step 2

If a range of cells has been selected, the range will be displayed in Step 2. To accept the range click **Next** to move onto Step 3. However, you may wish to see how your chart will look when the 'Series' is changed, ie swapping over the axis, from columns to rows etc.

A preview window appears above this information. If the chart does not appear correct, check that the data range is correct. If you need to amend the data range, click on the red

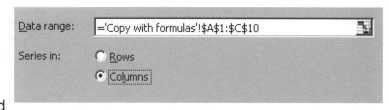

arrow to temporarily collapse the Chart Wizard box. Select the range(s) again on the worksheet and click the red arrow button to expand the **Chart Wizard**. Click on **Next**.

Step 3

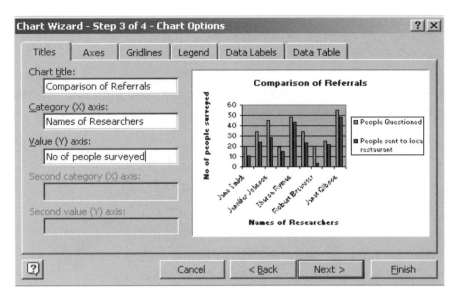

Tip: Move through the different sections of each tab by using the **Tab** key.

To move from one tab to another click **Ctrl+Tab**.

Step 3 of the wizard asks for information such as the **Titles** to appear on the chart. The Chart can have a main title, an X axis title and a Y axis title. The X axis is the horizontal axis and the Y axis is the vertical axis. These options may not be available for certain types of chart, such as a pie chart, which has no axis.

Other options in Step 3 include the **Legend** tab. The legend is the key on the chart to indicate what the coloured bars represent.

By removing the tick from the check box, the legend can be removed. You can also choose where the legend will appear.

The **Data Labels** tab will enable you to add data to the chart, such as the values or labels, to indicate what each bar represents. It is a good idea to spend a few minutes seeing what you do in this step of the wizard. The preview will show you what you have chosen.

T A S K

1. Open the **Research** workbook, select the **Copy with formulas** sheet.

2. Create a chart to compare how many people each researcher interviewed to how many were sent to the restaurant. To achieve this, highlight the data in cells **A1:C10** and create a column chart.

3. Give your chart a title which describes its outcome, ie **Comparison of Referrals**.

4. Label the Category (X) axis, **Names of Researchers**.

5. Label the Category (Y) axis, **No of people surveyed**.

6. Experiment with adding and removing data labels and a legend.

Continued in the next task box ...

Step 4

You can choose to display the chart on the current worksheet or as a separate sheet in your workbook.

An Embedded Chart (As object in) is a chart object that is placed on a worksheet and saved within that worksheet when the workbook is saved. This is useful when you want to view or print the chart with the data on the spreadsheet displayed. A chart object can be moved and resized in the same way other objects can be moved and resized.

A Chart Sheet (As new sheet) will appear on a seperate sheet in the workbook. Both charts are linked to the source data from the worksheet and are automatically updated when the worksheet data is updated.

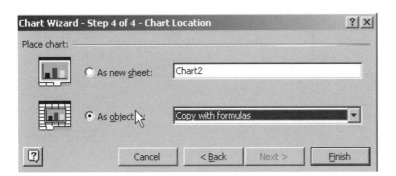

The second option is selected by default in step 4 of the wizard. To insert the chart as a new sheet, click on the radio button.

Click **Finish** to insert the chart.

To quickly insert a chart on a seperate sheet, select the cells and press **F11**.

T A S K	7.	*Insert the chart as an object in the worksheet* ***Copy with formulas***.
	8.	*Create another chart using the same information, placing this as a new sheet within the workbook. Name this sheet* ***Referrals Chart***.
		NB ***The next section covers moving and resizing charts.***

Figure 1

People Questionned	local restaurant	Price paid by restaurant	Total price paid by restaurant	
20	11	£4.31	£47.41	
34	24	£4.31	£103.44	
45	28	£4.31	£120.68	Commission earned
19	15	£4.31	£64.65	
48	43	£4.31	£185.33	

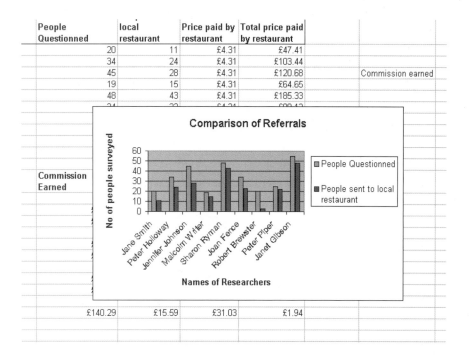

Commission Earned

| £140.29 | £15.59 | £31.03 | £1.94 | |

Figure 2

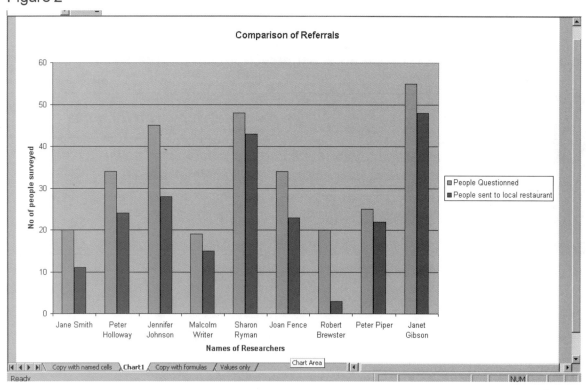

Moving And Resizing Charts

When a chart is inserted as an object on the worksheet, it may not appear in the correct position. Charts containing a lot of data may not be able to display all the data.

A chart can be resized. Click on the chart to select it. Point to one of the black handles around the chart. The mouse pointer will change to a double-headed black arrow. Click and hold the left mouse button and drag the handle to resize the chart. If you make the chart object larger, all data will be displayed.

To move the chart, point to the chart area itself. The mouse pointer will change to a four-headed black arrow. Click and hold the left mouse button and drag the chart to a new location on the worksheet.

A chart is made up of separate components, ie the Legend, the X and Y Axis labels etc. These components can also be moved, resized and even formatted on the chart. Click on the components to select them and drag in the same way as above.

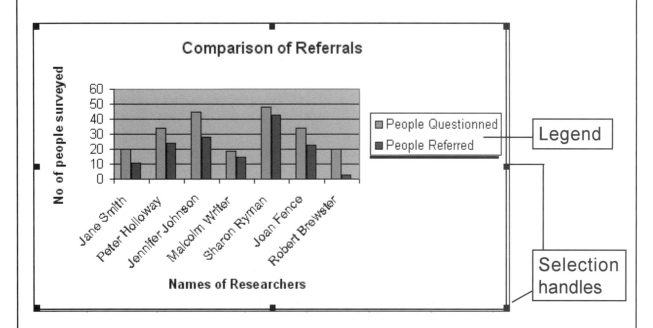

T	1.	Select the chart object within the worksheet *Copy with formulas* worksheet.
A		
S		
K	2.	Move the chart so that it is beside the worksheet data.
	3.	Increase the size of the chart so that all information within the chart is clearly visible.
	4.	Save the changes.

Editing A Chart

Charts can be modified to display different fonts, chart colours and text colours etc. You can also convert the chart to another type.

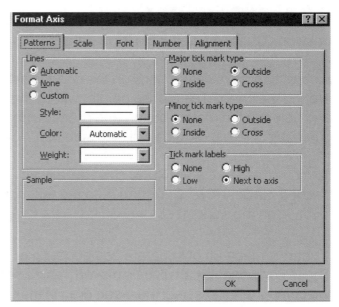

To format a component of the chart, point to it and double-click to open the appropriate dialogue box.

This dialogue box opens when you double-click on an axis.

Click on the **Font** tab to change the font attributes of the selected component. This is the same as the **Format Font** dialogue box.

The **Alignment** tab will enable you to change the orientation of text.

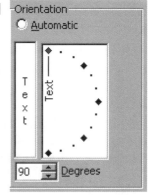

T		Using the worksheet **Referrals Chart**.
A		
S	1.	Format the font size of the text **Names of Researchers** to 8.
K		
	2.	Format the font size of the text **No of people surveyed** to 8.
	3.	Format the font size of the legend to 8, reposition it to the bottom right-hand corner.
	4.	Change the number of People Surveyed by Peter Holloway to 45 (cell **B3**) and the number referred to 40 (cell **C3**). View the chart and check that the data has updated.
	5.	Save the changes.
	6.	Print the worksheet.

Changing The Chart Type

Once a chart has been inserted, it is possible to change the way data is compared by changing the chart type.

For example, you have created a column chart of data, but now think that it would be better expressed as a line chart. To change the chart type, select the chart on the worksheet (selection handles will appear) or click on the chart sheet.

Click **Chart**, **Chart Type** from the menu bar. The **Chart Type** dialogue box will open.

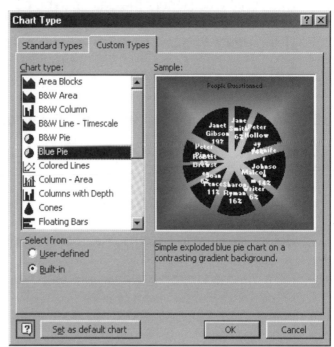

There are two tabs to select from: Standard Types and Custom Types.

Standard Types – select a chart type from the list on the left and a chart sub-type from the samples on the right.

Custom Types – click on a chart type in the list on the left to see a preview of what your chart will look like in that chart type.

T
A
S
K

1. *Ensure you are working on the **Copy with formulas** sheet on the **Research** workbook.*

2. *Change the chart type to a bar chart. In so doing, you may need to format the axis titles, resize the charts and change the font sizes.*

3. *Save the changes.*

4. *Select cells **A1:A10** and **C1:C10** (remember to hold down the **Ctrl** key) and create a pie chart.*

5. *Add a suitable title to the pie chart.*

6. *Show values on the pie chart.*

7. *Place as an object on the **Copy with formulas** sheet.*

8. *Reposition and resize both charts so that all data and the charts are visible on your worksheet (change the zoom settings to help achieve this).*

9. *Save the spreadsheet.*

Using Paste Special With Charts And Graphs

If you wish to create a chart that *will not* update if the data is changed, you will need to copy just the values to another area of the worksheet or to another worksheet using **Paste Special**.

1.   Select the cells required. Choose **Edit** on the menu bar and click **Copy** or click the **Copy** button on the Standard toolbar.

2.   Click on the cell where the data is to be copied.

3.   Using **Paste Special**, copy the values only.

4.   Create a chart from the copied data.

NB   You must update just the original data and not the copied values.

Printing The Chart

There are two options when printing charts:

-   Select the chart to print the chart only (or print the chart sheet)

-   Print the chart together with worksheet data

To print just a chart embedded on the worksheet, select the chart and click **Print**.

To print the complete worksheet showing the chart and source data, click on the worksheet and click **Print**.

TASK

1.   *Ensure you are working on the **Copy with formulas** sheet within the **Research** spreadsheet.*

2.   *Copy cells **A1:B10** and paste the values only to a blank part of the spreadsheet.*

3.   *Using the pasted values, create a suitable chart.*

4.   *Give the chart a title and label the X and Y axis.*

5.   *Format the chart appropriately. Check all the information is displayed, if not, resize the chart object and format the titles.*

6.   *Print the chart.*

7.   *Save the changes and close.*

CONSOLIDATION EXERCISE

1. Start a new blank workbook and key in the following data:

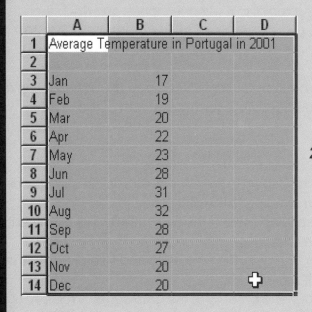

	A	B	C	D
1	Average Temperature in Portugal in 2001			
2				
3	Jan	17		
4	Feb	19		
5	Mar	20		
6	Apr	22		
7	May	23		
8	Jun	28		
9	Jul	31		
10	Aug	32		
11	Sep	28		
12	Oct	27		
13	Nov	20		
14	Dec	20		

2. Format column **B** to number, 0 decimal places.

3. Create a line chart on a separate sheet using appropriate titles and labels. Print a copy of the chart sheet and name the sheet **Line chart**.

Your chart should look similar to this:

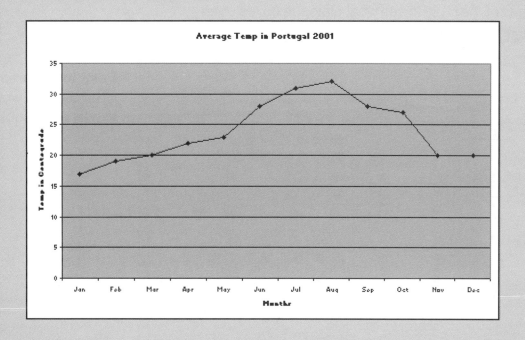

4. Save your spreadsheet as **Portugal**.

Formatting Charts

Every part of a chart can be formatted using the appropriate dialogue box. The quickest way to format an element of the chart is to point to it with the mouse and double-click. This will open the appropriate dialogue box where you can make changes to that part of the chart.

As you move around a chart, you will notice that screen tips pop up (in yellow boxes) to show you what you are pointing at. Double-click to format that part of the chart.

The following items can be formatted:

Chart Area - You can apply borders and shading to the chart area and set other properties.
Plot Area - You can apply borders and shading to the plot area.
Chart Title - You can change the font, style and size of the chart title and its alignment. You can also add borders and shading to a chart title.
Axes - You can change the scale of a value axis, the font, style and size of the axis labels, the number format of values and the alignment.
Data Series - You can change the colour and borders of the data series. You can change the order in which the series are displayed, add error bars and data labels. You can even change the gap between columns or bars and choose whether they should overlap.
Legend - You can apply borders and shading to a legend and change the font, style and size of the text in the legend. You can also choose the placement of the legend on the chart.

The best way to find out about the changes you can make to charts, is to experiment with a chart. Explore the options available in the **Chart** menu and double-click on different areas of the chart to see what dialogue boxes open.

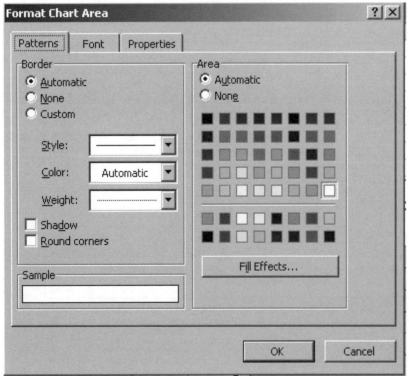

Point to the area of the chart that you would like to alter and double-click.

You can add a border and shading to the background of your chart. You can change the colour and font of the text on the chart.

In the **Format Chart Area** dialogue box, select a **Border** and **Area** colour. Alternatively, click **Fill Effects** button and choose **Gradient**, **Texture** or **Pattern** to use in the background of your chart. If you select the **Picture** tab and click **Select Picture**, you can insert a picture as the background to your chart.

Using the **Font** tab, you can change all the headings and labels to the same colour and/or font. If you wish to change them individually, double-click on each title separately.

When you double-click within the plot area, the **Format Plot Area** dialogue box will appear:

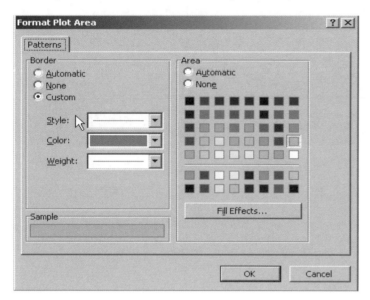

You can use this dialogue box to add borders and shading to the plot area of the chart. You can also click **Fill Effects** and add these effects (as above) to the plot area.

When you double-click on the data series of the chart, the **Format Data Series** dialogue box will appear.

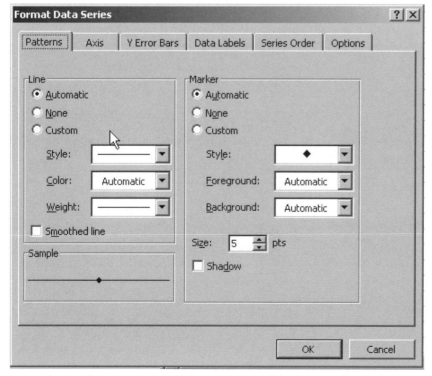

This dialogue box will vary according to the type of chart you have created.

It offers a number of different tabs.

Changes can be made to the colours of a line chart and data labels can be added.

You can change the colour of the gridlines and the scale of the chart by double-clicking on any gridline.

To format an axis on your chart, point to the axis and double-click.

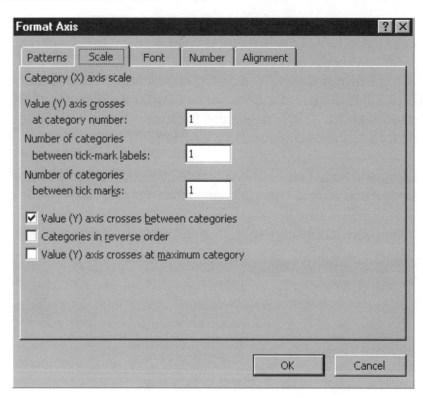

T
A
S
K

1. Ensure you are working on the **Portugal** workbook.

2. Delete information for all the months of the year and enter the following:

3	7-Jan	17
4	14-Jan	19
5	21-Jan	20
6	28-Jan	22

3. Notice how your line chart has changed. Double-click on the **Category Axis** and check the Major unit is 7 so that only the weekly dates appear.

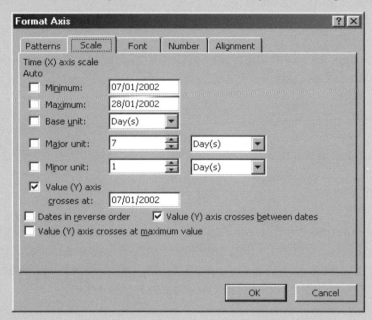

4. Change the **Y** axis so that the Minimum and Maximum values are **15** and **30**.

5. Check that your chart has now changed to incorporate the above changes.

6. Print a copy of the chart.

7. Save the changes to the spreadsheet.

8. Close the workbook.

Working With Objects

Importing Objects Into A Spreadsheet

To import is to 'bring' something into the application. An object can be data or a graphic created in another application, such as databases, word processed documents and images created in a graphics application.

When objects are imported, Excel will place the objects on the current worksheet. The objects will appear with selection handles around them which you can use for resizing and repositioning the object on the worksheet.

There are two choices when importing (inserting) an object into a workbook. The object can be linked or embedded.

Destination file

The destination file is the file that a linked or embedded object is inserted into.

Linked objects

Objects created in one file (the source file) and inserted into another file (the destination file) while maintaining a connection between the two files are called **Linked Objects**. The linked object in the destination file is automatically updated when the source file is updated. A linked object does not become part of the destination file.

Embedded objects

Objects created in one file (the source file) and inserted into another file (the destination file) with no connection between the two files are called **Embedded Objects**. When you double-click an embedded object, it opens in the application (source application) that it was created in. Any changes you make to the embedded object are reflected in the destination file. Changes made to the source file will not be reflected in the embedded object. An embedded object becomes part of the destination file.

Source file

The file in which information was created before becoming a linked or embedded object. When you update information in this source file, a linked object in the destination file is also updated.

Inserting a linked object is useful if you want to always view the latest data in the destination file. The object is a link to the original file.

Inserting An Object Into A Spreadsheet

Choose **Insert** on the menu bar and click **Object**. The following dialogue box appears:

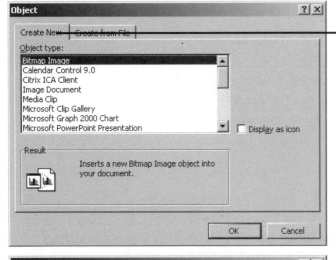

The **Create New** tab will be activated. Here an application can be selected and a new object created within the active workbook.

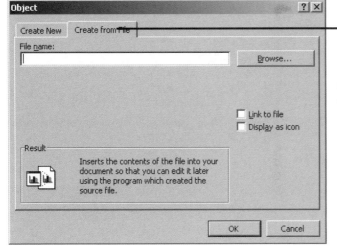

If the file that you wish to insert already exists, click on the **Create from File** tab.

The **Browse** button allows you to search for the file to be inserted as an object.

To locate the required file, click on **Browse** to open the **Browse** dialogue box. Locate the file, click to select it and click on the **Insert** button.

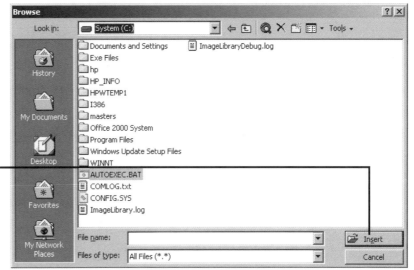

The path to the file will appear in the **Object** dialogue box.

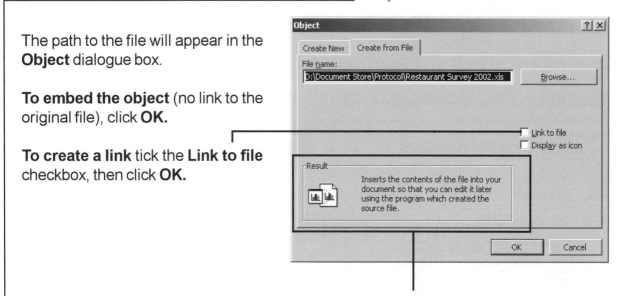

To embed the object (no link to the original file), click **OK.**

To create a link tick the **Link to file** checkbox, then click **OK.**

NB Notice in each section of the dialogue box, a Result section is displayed. This gives you information about what the result will be if the specified option is chosen.

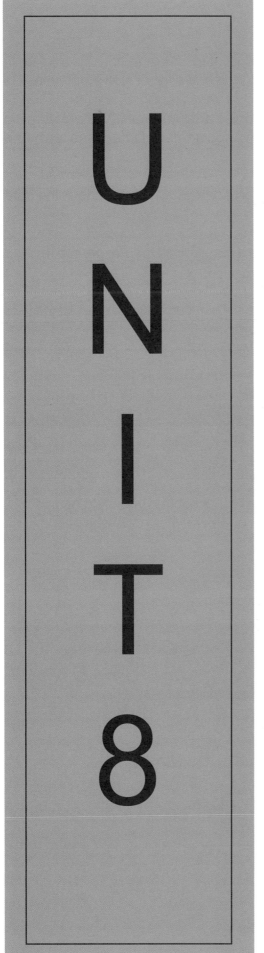

On completion of this unit, you will have learnt about and practised the following:

- **Creating A Data Form**

  - Sorting Data
  - Changing Excel's Defaults

- **Templates**

  - Creating Templates
  - Saving Templates

- **Find And Replace**

  - Using The Find Tool To Search For Spreadsheet Content
  - Using The Replace Tool To Change Spreadsheet Content

Creating A Data Form

A database is an organised collection (or list) of related information. Examples of databases include a telephone book, a library catalogue and a list of staff employees.

Excel refers to a database as a list and you can organise and manage the information so that it can be sorted, new information added, deleted and printed. Databases are made up of fields and records.

A **field** is a label (a column header) such as 'Name' or 'Address' which describes the data held in that column.

A **record** is one complete set of information such as a record held for one person, ie their name, address and telephone number.

You can add records to a list by typing directly into the cells once you have created the field names or you can use a **data form** to add new records.

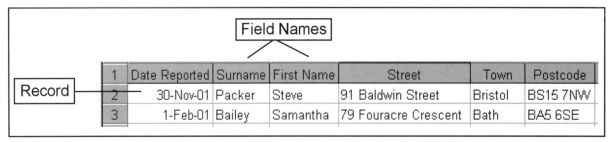

To use a data form to enter information, select the cells that contain your field names (headers). Choose **Data** on the menu bar and click on **Form**. If no data has been entered into your list, the following message will appear:

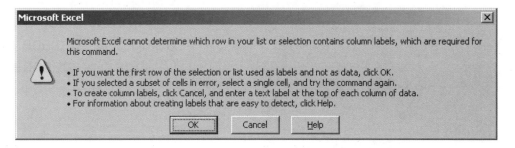

Click **OK** to create the data form.

The list of field names appears down the left side of the data form. Boxes used for entering information appear in the centre.

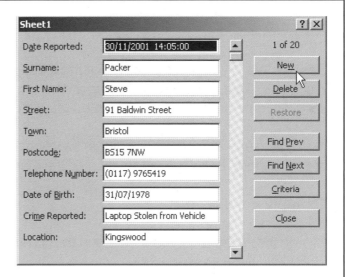

Using a data form is a more 'user friendly' way of entering information into a list or database.

The top right corner of the data form will show the number of records in the database or list.

The scroll bar in the centre of the data form enables you to scroll through the records in the database. You can use the buttons on the right side to create **New** records and **Delete** the current record. If you click on the **Criteria** button, you can type in search criteria (ie what you want to find and in which field). Use the **Find Prev** and **Find Next** buttons to carry out the search. The **Close** button will close the data form so that you can view the records on the worksheet.

TASK

1. Open the **Police Records** spreadsheet.

2. View the existing data using a data form. View the information it contains.

3. Click **New** and add the following details:

   26-Apr-01, John Fairman, 5 Goodman Lane, Bath, BA4 2VW, (0118) 4522212, 04/05/70, Vehicle Stolen, Blatherton.

4. Save changes made.

5. Click **Close**. The new details will show at the bottom of the list (database).

Sorting Data

Sorting data within a database is putting it into an order (eg ascending or descending, A-Z or Z-A). Data can be sorted using a single criteria or several criteria. Records can be sorted in date order alone or alphabetically and in date order.

If your field names (column headings) are formatted differently to the data in the list (ie bold or underlined), Excel will automatically use these as the field names for the sort.

To apply a quick sort:

Click in the column that you wish to sort the list by, ie Surname, Town etc (DO NOT SELECT THE COLUMN).

Click on the **Sort Ascending** or **Sort Descending** buttons on the Standard toolbar. The complete record is sorted by the current column.

To sort data, highlight the selection of data to be sorted and select **Data**, **Sort** from the menu bar. The **Sort** dialogue box will be displayed:

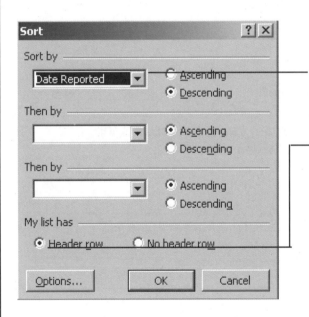

Use the drop-down arrow to decide which field name you wish to sort by first. (You can also choose Ascending A-Z or Descending Z-A.)

As your list has field names in Row A, the Header row box will be selected.

If yours does not have field names, the **No header row** box will be selected and the **Sort by** list would show Column letters, ie Column A, Column B etc.

(You can choose up to three levels of Sort in the dialogue box.)

T
A
S
K

1.   Sort the **Police Records** database by Surname in Ascending order.

2.   Print the spreadsheet, write on the printout '**Surname**'.

3.   Save the changes.

4.   Close the spreadsheet.

Changing Excel's Defaults

When you start a new workbook in Excel, the default number of worksheets available is 3. This can be changed. Click **Tools**, **Options** from the menu bar and click on the **General** tab.

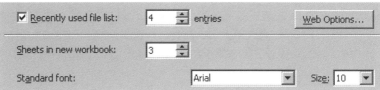

Locate **Sheets in new workbook** and change this value, using the up and down arrows, or by typing in a new value.

The **Recently used file list** enables you to choose how many of the last used files display at the bottom of the **File** menu. This is a quick way to open recently used files.

Click on **OK** to carry out these changes.

You can change the standard font and font size that new workbooks display.

After you carry out the changes and click **OK**, the following message will appear.

Click **OK**. (The changes will not take effect until the next time you launch Excel.)

T A S K	1. Create a new workbook. Make a note of the existing settings and then change them to: Recently used file list to 6 Sheets in new workbook to 10 Standard font to Times New Roman 12 2. Click **OK** and then exit from Excel. 3. Launch Excel again. 4. View the changes made. 5. Change the settings back to their original values. 6. Exit from Excel.

Templates

Creating Templates

A **template** is a workbook that contains text, formatting and formulae etc that you can use over and over again. Once you save a workbook as a template, it provides a framework for creating new workbooks without having to enter the same headings, images and formats.

T A S K.

*The market research company requires a template to include its name, address and logo on all its spreadsheets. Create a template spreadsheet and save it as **Market Research Template**.*

1. *Create a new blank workbook.*

2. *Type in the following data, beginning in cell **A1**.*

   Market Research Company Limited
   12 The Square
   Scarbury
   West Derbyshire
   WD1 4RR

   Tel: 01996 456789

3. *Merge and centre the heading across columns **A** to **I** and format the font to size 26.*

4. *Format the address to font size 14.*

5. *Insert a picture from the Microsoft Clip Art Gallery:*

   *Choose **Insert**, **Picture**, **Clip Art** and choose a picture of your choice. When the picture is selected, the drop-down menu appears:*

   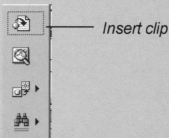 ——— *Insert clip*

   Insert the clip, resize it to 3cm x 3cm and move the picture so that it is under the right end of the company name.

   Continued in the next task box...

Saving Templates

When you are saving a spreadsheet to be used as a template or 'model', it is saved in a different format than a normal workbook. Normal spreadsheets are saved with the extension 'xls' as their file extension. If you save a spreadsheet as a template, it is saved as an 'xlt' file (ie E**x**cel **s**preadsheet and E**x**cel **t**emplate).

To save a spreadsheet as a template, choose **File**, on the menu bar and click **Save As**. The **Save As** dialogue box appears. Click on the drop-down arrow for **Save as type** and choose **Template (*.xlt)** from the list.

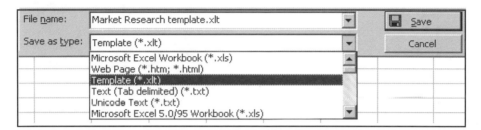

Give the template a name in the **File name** box.

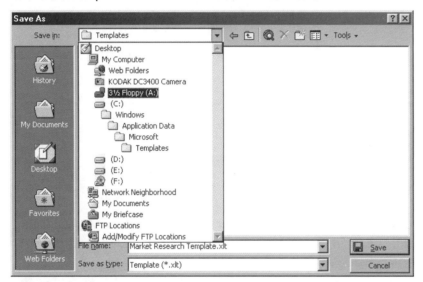

Select the location to save the file in from the **Save in:** drop-down list.

Click **Save** to save the template and then close it.

When you choose template as the **Save as type,** you will automatically be taken into the **Templates** folder. If you save your template into this folder, it will appear on the **General** tab of the **File, New** dialogue box.

To create a new spreadsheet using the template from the templates folder, choose **File**, **New** and you will see the template in the **General** section.

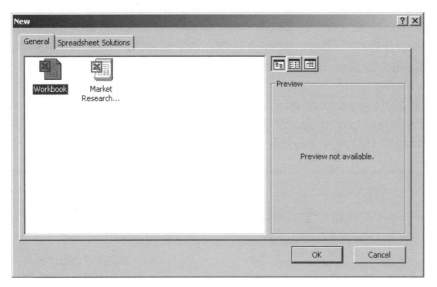

To create a new spreadsheet using a template from a floppy disk, choose **File**, **New** and select the **General** tab. Right-click the mouse button in an empty area of the window and select **Open** from the shortcut menu. Navigate to the floppy disk and locate the template.

Double-click the template icon and click **Cancel**. Your template is now open, ready for input.

T A S K

6. *Save the spreadsheet as a template to your floppy disk using the name* **Market Research Template**.

7. *Close the template. Reopen the template ready for use.*

8. *Open the* **Summary** *spreadsheet. You may receive a message (telling you that this workbook is linked to another). Click* **No** *(no changes have been made to the linked files).*

9. *Copy the data from the* **Summary** *spreadsheet into the template.*

10. *Save as* **New Summary** *and close all active workbooks.*

Find And Replace

Using The Find Tool To Search For Spreadsheet Content

Excel has a facility to find and replace data. This is useful when working with large spreadsheets with lots of data. Searches can be carried out to find specific text or numbers on the worksheet. The data can be replaced automatically once found. Cells that contain a specific type of data, such as a formula and cells whose contents do not match the active cell can also be found.

To activate **Find**, choose **Edit** on the menu bar and click **Find**. The following dialogue box will appear:

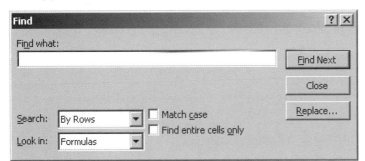

Type the data that you wish to find into the **Find what** box. Choose to search by rows or columns. Other options include looking in Formulas, Values or Comments (if they appear on the spreadsheet).

Match case will match the data exactly as typed in, eg if text is typed in uppercase in the **Find** dialogue box but appears on the sheet in lowercase or title case, the Find would not locate anything and the following message would appear:

To rectify this, click **OK** and retype the search criteria in the **Find what** box.

Click on **Find Next** to start the search. Once you have found the data, click on **Close** to close the Find dialogue box. To cancel a search at any time, press the **Esc** key on the keyboard.

Using The Replace Tool To Change Spreadsheet Content

To find data and replace it, choose **Edit** on the menu bar and click **Replace**. The following dialogue box will be displayed:

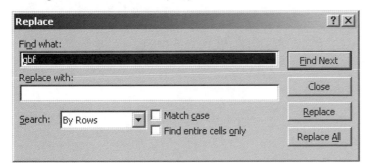

Type in the data that you want to find in the **Find what** box and the data you want to replace it with in the **Replace with** box. Choose whether you wish to search **By Rows** or **By Columns**.

Click on **Find Next** to start the search.

Click on **Replace** to replace the found data one at a time or **Replace All** to replace all the found data. If you wish to find data and delete it, leave the **Replace with** box blank.

CONSOLIDATION EXERCISE

You have been asked to analyse the ticket sales of the Cineshow cinema in Southington for the month of July and display various results from it.

1. Open the spreadsheet called **Ticket Sales**.

2. Some of the dates are in the wrong order. Sort the **Date** in ascending order.

3. Save the changes.

4. Create a new workbook. Set up a table as shown below:

	A	B	C	D	E	F
1	Ticket Sales					
2	Week ending	Average	Maximum	Minimum	Range	Average for Month
3	07-Jul					
4	14-Jul					
5	21-Jul					
6	28-Jul					

5. Save the new workbook as **Ticket Sales Analysed**.

6. Insert a footer containing your name, the file name and **Printout 1**.

7. Using the data from the **Ticket Sales** spreadsheet, work out the values for the **Average**, **Maximum** and **Minimum** columns within the **Ticket Sales Analysed** spreadsheet.

8. Subtract the Minimum from the Maximum to calculate the **Range** of ticket sales.

9. In cell F6 calculate the average sales for the month. Fill the cell with a suitable colour and apply borders.

10. On the same sheet, create an appropriate chart showing the variation of the maximum weekly ticket sales. Ensure the following formatting is applied:

   - Clear chart heading and axes titles.
   - Delete any unnecessary legends.
   - Format the background to a different colour, ensuring the chart details are clear.
   - Format any text to a smaller/bigger font to make sure it is legible.
   - Change the scale if this improves the output.

Continued in the next task box…

CONSOLIDATION EXERCISE

11   Arrange the chart and data so it fits on one sheet of paper.

12.   Print the spreadsheet and save the changes.

Example of how your chart may look:

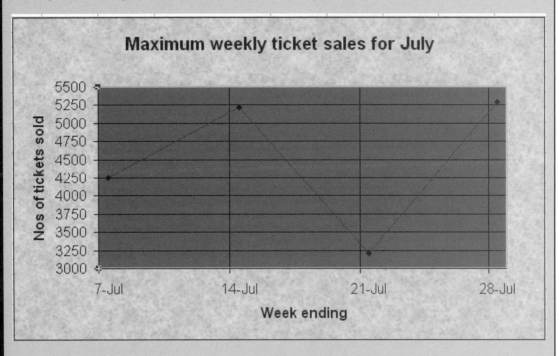

13.   Produce a screen print to show all the files you have created on your floppy disk.

APPENDIX

- **Microsoft Excel Help**
- **Keyboard Shortcuts**
- **Glossary of Terms**

©Tektra TEKSS2RP1102

Microsoft Excel Help

Microsoft Office has a comprehensive help system. There are four types of help:

- Context-sensitive help
- Office Assistant
- Contents
- Index

Context-sensitive help

This enables you to point at any part of the screen, including toolbars and menu bars, and be given information about its name and what it is used for. Choose **Help** on the menu bar and click **What's This?** Alternatively, press **Shift+F1**. Your mouse pointer will now have a question mark attached to it.

Click on the item that you would like to know more about. A hint box will appear:

> **Paste (Edit menu)**
>
> Inserts the contents of the Clipboard at the insertion point, and replaces any selection. This command is available only if you have cut or copied an object, text, or contents of a cell.

Office Assistant

The Office Assistant provides help and gives tips to enable you to accomplish your tasks.

Choose **Help** on the menu bar and click **Show the Office Assistant**, or click the **Office Assistant** button on the Standard toolbar.

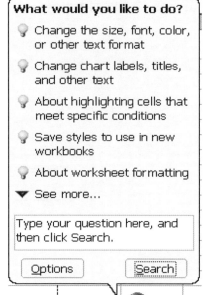

When you click on the Office Assistant, a pop-up menu will ask you to type in your question.

You can also click **Options** to change the settings of the Assistant.

To Hide the Office Assistant

Choose **Help** on the menu bar and click **Hide the Office Assistant** or right-click the mouse button on the Office Assistant and the shortcut menu will appear.

Click **Hide**.

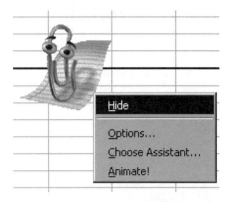

Right-click on the Office Assistant and click **Options.** The **Office Assistant** dialogue box will appear. In order to use the Contents and Index Help facility, you need to remove the tick from the check box **Use the Office Assistant**.

(If you click on the **Gallery** tab you can choose from a range of different Office Assistants.)

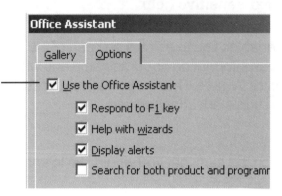

Contents

The Contents help section is similar to a reference library. Choose from a selection of book titles relating to topics, open them and choose further selections to refine your search. This is especially useful if you don't know the exact wording of the required feature. **Contents** allows you to browse through the selection.

To open Contents:

Choose **Help** on the menu bar.
Click **Microsoft Excel Help**.

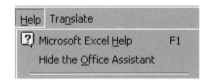

Remember, you must have the Office Assistant
turned off to be able to use Contents.

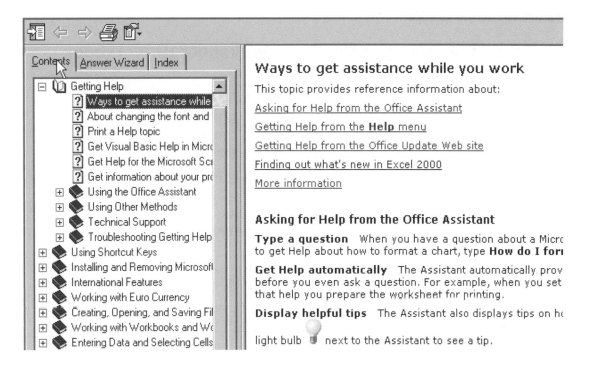

Index

The Index help section works like a search engine, ie you type in keywords or choose keywords from the list and select the topic particular to that word.

To open Index

Choose **Help** on the menu bar and click on **Microsoft Excel Help**. Click on the **Index** tab.

Type in the word(s) you wish to search for in the keywords box.

Click **Search**.

A list of topics will be displayed.

Click on a topic in the list to display the information on that topic on the right.

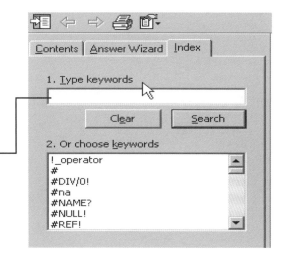

Keyboard Shortcuts

Keys for moving and scrolling in a worksheet or workbook

Arrow keys	Move one cell up, down, left, or right
Ctrl+arrow key	Move to the edge of the current data region
Home	Move to the beginning of the row
Ctrl+Home	Move to the beginning of the worksheet
Ctrl+End	Move to the last cell on the worksheet, which is the cell at the intersection of the right most used column and the bottom most used row (in the lower right corner), or the cell opposite the home cell, which is typically A1
Page Down	Move down one screen
Page Up	Move up one screen
Alt+Page Down	Move one screen to the right
Alt+Page Up	Move one screen to the left
Ctrl+Page Down	Move to the next sheet in the workbook
Ctrl+Page Up	Move to the previous sheet in the workbook

Glossary

Absolute cell reference	A cell reference in a formula that will always refer to the same cell, even when the formula is copied to a different part of the worksheet.
Active cell	The cell currently selected and shown by a heavy border.
Alignment	The horizontal placement of cell contents. eg left, centre or right.
Ascending order	Data organised from A to Z or 0 to 9.
Attribute	A styling feature such as bold, italics and underlining that can be applied to cell contents.
AutoCalculate area	The area in the status bar that displays the sum or function of the values in the selected range.
AutoFill	A feature that automatically enters a list into a range of cells.
Automatic calculation	The default option on the **Calculation** tab of the **Options** dialogue box that tells Excel to recalculate the formulae automatically when you change the value in a cell.
AutoSum	The feature in the Standard toolbar which offers the quickest way of adding a column or row of figures.
Block	Any rectangular group of cells indicated by the addresses of the top left and bottom right cells.
Border	The edge of a selected area of a worksheet. Lines and colours can be applied to borders.
Cell	An individual box used to store data.
Cell address	Consists of 2 coordinates (the column letter followed by the row number).
Cell pointer	The highlighted rectangle around a cell that indicates the active cell.
Check box	A square box in a dialogue box that can be clicked to turn an option on or off.
Clear	A command on the **Edit** menu used to erase a cell's contents, ie formatting or all contents.
Constant input data	The data that is entered into the spreadsheet that does not change, ie labels, headings, titles.
Data form	A data entry window used to view or add records to a list.

Data input form	A paper-based form that data can be recorded onto before being entered into the spreadsheet.
Data label	The text that appears above a data marker on a chart.
Data processing	Excel will process the data to produce output data from the formulae and functions.
Data series	The information, usually numbers or values, that Excel uses to plot a chart.
Delete	The command that removes cell contents from a worksheet.
Descending order	Data organised from Z to A or 9 to 0.
Dialogue box	The window that displays when you choose a command followed by an ellipsis (…).
Embedding	The process of inserting a copy of the original object in the destination document. An embedded object can be edited from within the destination program, using the source program's tools and commands. It retains no connection with the original object.
Extension	A code attached to the end of the filename which identifies the type of file, ie **.xls - Excel workbook**.
File	In Excel, this is known as a workbook.
File properties	Relates to the properties of the workbook file such as its name, size, author, type etc.
Fill handle	Small square in the lower-right corner of the active cell used to copy cell contents.
Find and replace	A command used to find one set of criteria and replace it with new information.
Font	A typeface used to print or display text.
Footer	Information that appears at the bottom of every page of a document, worksheet or workbook.
Format	The appearance of text and numbers in a spreadsheet cell.
Formula	A set of instructions entered in a cell to perform numeric calculations.
Formula bar	The area below the menu bar and above the workspace that displays entries in the active cell.
Frozen panes (freeze panes)	Columns or rows that have been fixed on the screen. They remain in one place enven when you scroll through the worksheet.

Function	Special pre-defined commands that provide a shortcut for commonly used calculations, ie SUM, AVERAGE, MIN, MAX, COUNT, IF.
Graphic object	A picture such as a drawing, logo or photograph.
Header	Information that appears at the top of every page of a document, worksheet or workbook.
Headings	Also known as labels. Define the content of columns or rows below or to the right.
Hidden data	Confidential data that exists on the worksheet but is not visible on screen.
Import	To bring a file from another program or another workbook into Excel.
Input data	Data that is entered into the worksheet. Can be constant input data or variable input data.
Insertion point	Blinking I-Beam that appears in the formula bar during entry and editing.
Label	Also known as the heading. Any textual cell entry.
Landscape orientation	Printing on a page whose dimensions are longer horizontally than vertically.
Linking	When a copy of the original object is inserted in the destination document but a connection is retained between the copy and the original. A linked object is updated automatically when the data in the original changes.
Locked cells	Cells that are protected so that their contents cannot be changed.
Macro	A set of recorded keystrokes or commands that tell the program how to perform a series of tasks.
Manual calculation	An option on the **Calculation** tab of the **Options** dialogue box that allows you to determine when the formulae in the worksheet are calculated.
Name	A name assigned to a selected cell or range in a worksheet.
Order of precedence	Also known as BODMAS, the order in which Excel calculates parts of a formula: (1) exponents, (2) multiplication and division and (3) addition and subtraction.
Page break preview	Allows you to view and change page breaks manually in the **Print Preview** window.

Paste Special	A command that enables you to paste formulae as values, styles or cell contents.
Plot area	The main area of a chart containing the plotted and formatted chart data and chart axes.
Portrait mode	The normal alignment of paper, with the vertical side being the longest.
Protection	An option that prevents cells from being altered.
Range	A selected group of adjacent cells.
Relative cell reference	Used to indicate a relative position in the worksheet. When you copy and move formulae from one area of the worksheet to another, Excel automatically changes the column row and numbers to reflect the new position.
Sheet	A term used for a worksheet.
Sort	To rearrange rows or a worksheet in a particular order.
Status bar	The bar near the bottom of the screen that provides information about the tasks Excel is performing or about any current selections.
Tab	A description at the bottom of each worksheet that identifies it in a workbook.
Validation	A command that allows you to specify what data is acceptable for a range of cells. Can also be used to manually check that formulae in worksheets are correct by using a calculator.
Value	A numeric value in a worksheet.
Variable input data	Data entered into a worksheet that changes from day to day, month to month etc.
Wizard	A series of dialogue boxes that lists and describes all Excel functions and assists the user in function or chart creation.
Workbook	A collection of related worksheets contained within a single file.
Worksheet	An electronic spreadsheet that contains 256 columns and 65,536 rows.
X-axis	The horizontal axis in a chart on which categories are plotted.
Y-axis	The vertical axis in a chart on which values are plotted.
Zoom	Enables the user to focus on a larger or smaller part of the worksheet in print preview.